THE ECSTASY OF BEING

THE COLLECTED WORKS OF JOSEPH CAMPBELL

More titles forthcoming

THE ECSTASY OF BEING

MYTHOLOGY AND DANCE

Joseph Campbell

EDITED AND WITH A FOREWORD BY
NANCY ALLISON, CMA

New World Library
Novato, California

New World Library
14 Pamaron Way
Novato, California 94949

Text design by Tona Pearce Myers

Library of Congress Cataloging-in-Publication Data

Names: Campbell, Joseph, 1904–1987, author.
Title: The ecstasy of being : mythology and dance / Joseph Campbell.
Description: Novato, California : New World Library, [2017] | Includes
     bibliographical references and index.
Identifiers: LCCN 2017030933 | ISBN 9781608683666 (alk. paper)
Subjects: LCSH: Modern dance--Philosophy. | Dance--Mythology.
Classification: LCC GV1783 .C38 2017 | DDC 792.8--dc23
LC record available at https://lccn.loc.gov/2017030933

First paperback printing, July 2023
ISBN 978-1-60868-889-0
Printed in Canada on 100% postconsumer-waste recycled paper

New World Library is proud to be a Gold Certified Environmentally Responsible Publisher. Publisher certification awarded by Green Press Initiative. www.greenpressinitiative.org

10   9   8   7   6   5   4   3   2   1

To Shirley Wimmer, Gladys Bailin, and Marcia Sakamoto,
who first opened my eyes to the magic of modern dance
and without whom I never would have met Jean and Joe.
—Nancy Allison, CMA, editor

CONTENTS

ABOUT THE COLLECTED WORKS OF
JOSEPH CAMPBELL

———————•———————

AT HIS DEATH in 1987, Joseph Campbell left a significant body of published work that explored his lifelong passion, the complex of universal myths and symbols that he called "Mankind's one great story." He also left, however, a large volume of unreleased work: uncollected articles, notes, letters, and diaries, as well as audio- and videotape-recorded lectures.

The Joseph Campbell Foundation—founded in 1990 to preserve, protect, and perpetuate Campbell's work—has undertaken to create a digital archive of his papers and recordings and to publish The Collected Works of Joseph Campbell.

THE COLLECTED WORKS OF JOSEPH CAMPBELL
Robert Walter, Executive Editor
David Kudler, Managing Editor

EDITOR'S FOREWORD

"ART IS THE FUNNEL through which spirit is poured into life,"
Joseph Campbell often said.[1] He believed deeply that art, like
mythology, has the power to open the contemporary, individual
mind to a direct experience of the timeless, transcendent wisdom of the universe, a wisdom based in the body and visited in
our dreams. According to Campbell, the artist's job is to create
"significant forms" that stir the modern, fractured psyche, "offering to consciousness an aesthetic object while ringing, simultaneously, undertones in the unconscious."[2]

Campbell's philosophy of art was deeply shaped by his trav-
els in Europe from 1924 to 1929, where he was introduced to the
literature of James Joyce and Thomas Mann; the paintings of
Cézanne, Picasso, and Paul Klee; the work and teaching of the
sculptor Antoine Bourdelle; and the groundbreaking psychological theories of Sigmund Freud and Carl Jung. Through this
heady brew of different yet related influences, Campbell eventually came to his belief that "the individual artist must study
the psychological effects produced by the various devices of his
particular craft" and that "these devices must then be associated with their appropriate elements of myth."[3] In this way, the
artist fulfills the task of pitching the individual psyche beyond
fear or hope to the "wonder of the world-harmony that keeps

in circulation (whether life be sorrowful or gay) the spheres of outer space, the electrons of the atom, and the juices of the living earth."[4]

Throughout his life, Campbell patiently explicated the rigorous standards and defining characteristics of what he, following James Joyce, called "proper art," art that stills the chattering mind and by means of its wholeness and harmonic rhythm illumines the arrested mind with the radiance of beauty.[5] With wit and warmth he inspired generations of young writers, poets, painters, sculptors, musicians, composers, actors, directors, and filmmakers to seek radiance in their artistic meditations. But as can be seen in this small volume, he had a special passion for choreographers and dancers.

We know very little about Campbell's earliest musings on the art of dance. We do know that as a child of just five or six, he had a life-altering experience when his father took him and his brother, Charlie, to *Buffalo Bill's Wild West Show* at Madison Square Garden. There, Campbell "became fascinated, seized, obsessed, by the figure of a naked American Indian with his ear to the ground, a bow and arrow in his hand, and a look of special knowledge in his eyes."[6] Did he perhaps also get his first glimpse there of the spiritually organized colors, forms, and rhythms of Native American dance?

Campbell Sr. also enjoyed what he called "good shows" and perhaps took Joe and Charlie to these vaudeville-style shows, too.[7] More than likely the young boys saw amazing African American tap dancers, as well as female chorus line dancing typical of the era. Stephen and Robin Larsen's biography, *A Fire in the Mind: The Life of Joseph Campbell*, documents that Campbell was a very good musician and a wonderful social dancer, but we don't know if he picked up the steps and style of the various dances by watching or by learning them through instruction, thereby developing an appreciation for some of the formal aspects of dance.

Campbell never mentions in his voluminous journals or

correspondence that he saw a ballet, either as a boy in New York or as a young man on any of his European trips between 1924 and 1929. During that time Diaghilev's Ballets Russes and the students of Rudolf von Laban—most notably Mary Wigman, the leading figure of German Expressionist dance—were performing regularly. So, too, were the Americans Isadora Duncan and Ruth St. Denis, yet there is no record of Campbell having seen them, or any of the other dance artists who were revolutionizing the art form during this period.

But in 1937, something happened that changed his understanding of dance altogether. At that time, Campbell was living the life he had dreamed up for himself, teaching comparative literature at the all-female Sarah Lawrence College with plenty of time on the side to continue his reading and study of world mythology. The same year he arrived, a young woman named Jean Erdman began her studies there, too.

Born and raised in Honolulu, Erdman grew up dancing hula at family parties and picnics almost as soon as she could walk. The daughter of Dr. John Pinney Erdman, a Protestant minister, and Marion Dillingham, a member of one of the major industrialist families of Hawaii, Jean attended the exclusive Punahou School, where she learned Isadora Duncan–style interpretive dance.[8] After a year spent at Miss Hall's School for Girls in Pittsfield, Massachusetts, where her intellect was ignited but her mind was troubled by the prevailing Puritanical attitude toward dance—she was disciplined for teaching hula to her classmates—she arrived at Sarah Lawrence full of youthful enthusiasm and a questing mind.[9]

Erdman dove into the dramatic, percussive dance technique taught there by modern dance pioneer Martha Graham and members of her company, and she continued her study at the Bennington Dance Festival during the summers. She also studied comparative religion and Irish culture and theater.[10] By her junior year, Erdman was committed to a life in dance and wanted to expand the breadth of her studies to include philosophy and aesthetics. Judging from her friends' descriptions of his classes, Erdman decided that Professor Campbell, heartthrob of the campus, was the ideal tutor for her interests, and she asked him for a private conference course. Self-selected private tutorial courses were a distinguishing feature of the program at Sarah Lawrence.

A chance encounter at the library on a rainy night turned into an interview at Campbell's office where, as the story goes, Campbell asked her, "What do you want to study?"

"I want to study aesthetics. I want to study Pluto," she replied.

"Pluto?" he asked. "You mean Plato!"

Despite her error (or Freudian slip), Campbell agreed to the tutorial as long as Erdman also attended his lecture course on Thomas Mann, which included reading assignments on Schopenhauer, Kant, and Nietzsche. Erdman was happy to comply.[11]

So, much to the envy of the entire campus, the dashing scholar and the beautiful dancer met every Tuesday from 12:30 to 1:30 to discuss art and philosophy. By the end of the semester, neither wanted the relationship to end. But Erdman would not be returning to campus the next year; instead, she was taking a trip around the world with her family. As a parting gift, Campbell gave her a copy of Oswald Spengler's *The Decline of the West*, knowing that she would need to stay in touch with him in order to understand it. As her parting gift, Erdman invited Campbell to see her perform at Bennington later that summer.[12]

What he saw there was not only the talent and beauty of his special student, but a whole new evolving art form, rooted in a glorious exploration of the possibilities of the human body. Here was a whole cadre of young choreographers—Martha Graham, Doris Humphrey, Charles Weidman, Hanya Holm—searching for original aesthetic forms through which to express their keen observations of the human condition, both inner and outer. Here was a field where Campbell could explore his burgeoning theory of the relationship of myth to aesthetic form and psychological structures.[13] Here was a dancer, Jean Erdman, with whom he could share his passion for art, myth, and a soul-directed life.

After Erdman left to join her family in Honolulu, the two continued their dialogue through a correspondence that grew ever more intimate as Jean traveled around the world. While Erdman experienced a physical journey, Campbell traversed the planet through the power of his imagination, elucidating for his beloved, as he would for so many others, the life-enhancing magic of the mythic symbols of the peoples and places of the earth. By the time their shared journey was complete, they had imagined together a life dedicated to love where "the walls of separateness are completely surpassed, and the embrace yields not pleasure but fulfillment, not children but self-realization, not the satisfaction of desire but the experience of eternity, not passion and possession but power and control."[14]

The couple married on May 5, 1938, in a simple ceremony officiated by Erdman's father in New York City. After a weekend honeymoon in Woodstock, New York, Erdman began rehearsing as a member of Martha Graham's company and Campbell returned to teaching at Sarah Lawrence. They rented a two-room apartment in New York City's Greenwich Village that would be their primary residence for the rest of their lives.

At first, Jean toured frequently with Graham, returning to Bennington for intensive rehearsal periods and choreographic study with Graham's musical director, the composer Louis Horst. Campbell was a welcome addition to the artistic exchange there, stimulating Graham with his profound insights. The friendship he forged with Horst, who was also the founding editor of *Dance Observer* magazine, resulted in Campbell's first published writing on aesthetic philosophy.

Campbell also formed a friendship with the composer John Cage. According to Erdman, they were all at a New Year's Eve party in 1942 when Cage suggested, somewhat coyly to

Campbell, that she and Merce Cunningham, also a member of Graham's company at that time, collaborate on a concert together at the Arts Club of Chicago. Eager to help Erdman develop her own creative voice, Campbell encouraged the project. Despite a negative reception by the local press, the project had the desired effect of launching Erdman into a life as an independent creative artist.[15]

Freed of the demands of Graham's creative process, the couple adopted their own rigorous schedule that allowed them plenty of time to work independently and also time together to share their discoveries and questions. Breakfast became a sacred ritual where Joe read aloud to Jean every word he wrote. She responded to the content, rhythm, and flow of his text.[16] When Jean was creating new work, Joe visited her studio to respond to her physical explorations from his deep well of mythological associations, often suggesting names for her dances.

As Campbell continued his studies of comparative mythology, Erdman began a comparative study of Western theatrical dance forms and the traditional dance styles she had seen on her trip around the world, along with new ones she continued to learn. Through this study she developed her own approach to dance technique, one that aimed to "give each dancer a completely articulate instrument, not limited by personal style."[17] She began teaching and performing and was soon touring again throughout the United States, now in her own concerts and teaching residencies.

Meanwhile, Campbell began to be published: the first was his introduction to the first title in the Bollingen series, *Where the Two Came to Their Father: A Navaho War Ceremonial Given by Jeff King*, illustrated by Maud Oakes (1943); then, *A Skeleton Key to Finnegans Wake* with Henry Morton Robinson (1944); and finally, his first complete statement of his long-gestating theory of the hero's journey, *The Hero with a Thousand Faces* (1949). He also edited Heinrich Zimmer's posthumous works, *Myths and Symbols in Indian Art and Civilization* (1946) and *The*

King and the Corpse (1948), as well as three Eranos yearbooks for the Bollingen series. Somehow between 1944 and 1950, he also found time to write the seven articles for the *Dance Observer* that open the first section of this book.

This highly productive period in Erdman and Campbell's lives culminated in 1954 and 1955 with Campbell's yearlong tour of India and the Far East. It was his first physical experience of many of the places he had described to Jean on her world tour with her parents seventeen years ago. That same year, Erdman, now also the director of the dance program at Bard College, went on her own solo world tour. She intersected with Campbell for just five weeks in India and a month in Japan before they returned to New York together.[18] They both embraced the hectic, busy lifestyle that often kept them miles apart, but wherever they were, they continued, through letters and telegrams, their intense dialogue that so nourished them both.

As time went on, they collaborated ever more directly. Beginning in the mid-1950s, they worked together to transform James Joyce's *Finnegans Wake* from a novel, one told from the perspective of the male barkeeper Humphrey Chimpden Earwicker, into an avant-garde dance theater piece that reflected the perspective of the main female character, Anna Livia Plurabelle, Joyce's modern incarnation of the divine feminine principle. Erdman choreographed, directed, and danced all the aspects of Anna Livia from young woman to old crone to the rain itself, which becomes the River Liffey flowing through the heart of Dublin. *The Coach with the Six Insides*, as they called her dance theater piece, premiered at the Village South Theater in Greenwich Village on November 26, 1962. It ran for 114 performances and received the Obie and Vernon Rice Awards (now known as the Drama Desk Awards) for outstanding achievement in theater. Following the first New York season, the piece began a world tour, including engagements at the Festival dei Due Mundi in Spoleto, Italy; the Théâtre des Nations in Paris; the Dublin Arts Festival in Ireland; and the Sogetsu Kaikan in

Tokyo. Three other North American tours as well as another New York season in 1967 followed. In 1964 the work was featured on the CBS *Camera Three* series. In 1966 WNET Channel 13 produced an interview with both Erdman and Campbell called *A Viewer's Guide to the Coach with the Six Insides*.

In 1972, when Campbell retired from Sarah Lawrence and Erdman had just gained greater artistic and financial success from her Tony-nominated choreography for Joseph Papp's Broadway production of *The Two Gentlemen of Verona*, they founded the Theater of the Open Eye together. Taking the Egyptian Eye of Horus, the eye to the eternal realm, as its symbol, the Open Eye was a home for mythopoetic dance-based theater incorporating arts and culture from around the world. Their first production was *Moon Mysteries*, three Irish Noh plays for dancers by W. B. Yeats, and over the next fifteen years, the Open Eye presented or produced over one hundred works of traditional and experimental dance and theater. Some were directed and choreographed by Erdman, others by the dancers, actors, musicians, and designers of the Open Eye company or by invited guests. It was also the home for *Realms of the Creative Spirit*, a series of weekend lectures by Campbell that became wildly popular with the whole company and the general public.

I joined the Open Eye in 1976 and remember vividly being mesmerized by Joe's incantatory voice as images of mythological symbols danced on the walls of the studio during those magical weekend lectures. Being part of that company was to be part of an artistic family that was on a constant tour of the world. I danced *en pointe* as an attendant to the Virgin Queen in *A Full Moon in March* and barefoot as a nymph, manipulating a silk "ocean," in *The Only Jealousy of Emer*, two of the three plays that comprise *Moon Mysteries*. I danced and played the *ogan* as a congregant in Teiji Ito's *Haitian Suite*, and I was tormented by monsters as Wahini O'mao, the spirit of woman, in *The Shining House: A Dance-Opera of Pagan Hawaii*, the last of Jean's Total Theater works. Company members were also encouraged to create our own works. Jean and Joe were always available to watch a rehearsal and offer insightful feedback.

I was just as mesmerized by the experience of dancing the role of the Youthful Virgin, the role Erdman had originally choreographed for herself, in her 1945 trio *Daughters of the Lonesome Isle*, which she remounted in 1977. The inventiveness and rhythmic complexity of the choreography, an amalgam of world dance from Hawaiian hula to Brazilian samba, set to John Cage's score on fully prepared piano, was simply breathtaking. For the next sixteen years, I worked closely with Jean re-creating her early dance repertory for concerts and for the three-part video archive *Dance and Myth: The World of Jean Erdman*.

During the last years of his life, Campbell remained active as a guest lecturer and teacher, often at the Esalen Institute in Big Sur, California, or leading groups to important cultural sites abroad. By that time, he and Jean had bought a two-room apartment on the Diamond Head end of Waikiki Beach, where life was quieter and he could concentrate on writing his final major opus, *Historical Atlas of World Mythology* (1983–88) and the short book *The Inner Reaches of Outer Space: Metaphor as Myth and as Religion* (1986). At the same time he was the subject of Stuart Brown and Phil Cousineau's independent film *The Hero's Journey*. On their many trips between Hawaii and New York, Campbell and Erdman often stopped in Marin County, California, where Campbell and Bill Moyers sat for hours at a time at George Lucas's Skywalker Ranch filming the interviews that would become the PBS television series *The Power of Myth*.

With a schedule like that, it's no surprise that the second part of this volume, the short book "Mythology and Form in the Performing and Visual Arts," remained unfinished at the time of Campbell's death in 1987. It's also no surprise that this small volume on modern dance, his final elucidation of the interrelationship between mythology, psychology, and aesthetic form, is a kind of love poem to Erdman, his muse and life partner during the glorious journey of an inspired and inspiring life.

A lot has changed in the dance world since 1987. I have no doubt that Campbell would be even more amazed to see a modern dance concert today than he was when he saw his first in 1937. But I also have no doubt that Campbell's small volume, which is an elegant account of the early days of modern dance by an ardent admirer participating fully in the struggles and triumphs of its unfolding, will be an enduring source of fructifying wisdom for generations of artists yet to be born.

This collection is divided into two parts. Part 1 contains seven articles and one transcribed lecture previously published between 1944 and 1978. For each, information concerning the specific date and place of publication is in the endnotes. Spelling, references, and footnotes appear exactly as they were originally published except where updated to bring them into accord with current style and the rest of the Collected Works series.

The second half of the book, "Mythology and Form in the Performing and Visual Arts," is an unpublished manuscript. With the exception of two paragraphs at the beginning of chapter 13, it was generally a clean manuscript, with very few discernible typographical errors. How much Campbell may have wanted to change is not known, so with the exception of the two aforementioned paragraphs and obvious typographical errors, I have left it unchanged. All of Campbell's footnotes and references have been checked.

Many facts, particularly those related to Jean Erdman and her colleagues' careers, probably remained unchecked at the time of Campbell's death. I have changed any incorrect dates and titles that I was able to verify from research in published sources and primary source material at the New York Public Library Dance Research Collection. Where multiple interpretations appeared, I have included the possible variations in the endnotes.

Throughout, Campbell's original footnotes have been moved to the endnotes.

In addition, in accordance with the style of the Collected Works of Joseph Campbell series, spelling of some words has been changed to reflect more accepted modern usage (such as Stravinsky, Nijinsky, Kṛṣṇa, Śiva, and so on).

—NANCY ALLISON, CMA

FIGURE 1. Modern dance (South Korea, 2009)

PART I

ARTICLES AND LECTURES
(1944–1978)

FIGURE 2. Dance instructor (United States, 1943)

Betwixt the Cup
and the Lip (1944)[1]

HAS ANYONE ELSE EVER SUFFERED from this feeling that has been affecting me at concerts? After all these years, it is not a nice thing to have to say; nevertheless, now that it comes to putting words to paper, there the feeling is, there it has long resided, and it will out.

My first glimpse of the world of the Modern Dance was at a technique demonstration at the Bennington Summer School. Perhaps it was the suddenness of it all—but it seemed to me I was beholding a revelation of the Mankind of the Future. With an affirmation that came throbbing from a zone of inexhaustible life-abundance, those young students made visible, through the form and sweep of the human body, something of the potency of the pulsation of the blood and the all-generating throb of time. The dead weight of circumstance, the accidents of the hour and the place, the imperfections of the flesh which condemn the majority of us to lumber along like beavers on the ground, dropped away, and there was Man, unshelled and glorious, in the full agony of life. The spirit was transported beyond the reach of words. Movement, meaning, and feeling were identical: verbalization would have been inane. I was beholding bodies hurled about by the volcano-fires of the throbbing abyss out of which we all have popped—out of which the worlds have popped, out of which have popped the spinning demons of the atom and the galaxies of the night. I tell you, it was something. It was immense.

But then, somewhat later, I attended my first concert: a succession of sketches illustrating the past and present of the United States of America, certain, didactic, and commiserative compositions around themes taken from the daily press, a few little giggle-pieces in a satiric vein, an attempt to illustrate a well-known theme out of Dr. Sigmund Freud's *General Introduction to Psychoanalysis*, and a pretty little musical arrangement (A-B-A) of some six or seven movement-devices. I must say, had it not been for the last, I should have thought myself wandered into the Modern Library. The Muse Terpsichore had donned her uncle's spectacles and whiskers. Every movement had been brought to subserve some momentous (yet somehow stale and familiar) philosophical thesis. All the butter was in the lesson, the moral. Whither oh whither those wonderful dynamisms, suggestive powers, and ineffable experiences of the simply overwhelming technique demonstration? I have been searching these seven years.

For the dance, of all the arts, is perhaps the least well adapted to subtle, or even persuasive, social criticism; and though it can be employed as a chocolate-coating for the popularization of scientific paragraphs and timely political *pronunciamentos*, it cannot operate creatively either in the laboratory or in the senate. The serious work in science, scholarship, and legislation is not accomplished to the tap of the tom-tom; the saraband cannot compete with the stump for votes. We are forced to wonder: is the Modern Dancer really comfortable and does she feel herself completely realized in this role of Drum Majorette? Having beheld that Bennington technique demonstration, I cannot think so. The Modern Dance, in its inception at any rate, must have been a considerable expression of life-power, life-courage, and the ecstasy of being. Where does it all disappear to, between the moment of the technique class and that of the stage?

Now, perhaps it is too much to ask—what I am asking. Perhaps only a semidivine genius, capable of dancing through all the agonies of modern existence, would possess the power to open out into a full-fledged choreography the sublimely heroic implications of the primary techniques of that first, transporting demonstration. For the dancer would have to create, not in protest against the inevitables of existence, nor again in wide-eyed utopianism or in avoidance of the life-issues of our day, but in full consciousness of the terror, and in ecstatic affirmation, nevertheless. From earliest times, the dancer has been the human symbol of life-indestructible. The Dionysos-dance of annihilation is at the same time the dance of the fire of creation: the oxidizing fire of the interior of the living cell. Need it be pointed out that life is a process; process, change; change, painful: pain-and-death the other face of joy-and-birth? It is a basic principle of aesthetics that art is produced not out of fear, or out of hope, but out of an experience transcending the two, holding the two in balance, and revealing the wonder of the world-harmony that keeps in circulation (whether life be sorrowful or gay) the spheres of outer space, the electrons of the atom, and the juices of the living earth. These our times are particularly difficult; the more need, therefore, for the basic affirmation of an uncorrupted art.

Unfortunately, the Modern Dance, as season follows season, steadily is drifting farther and farther from the drumbeat of the demiurgic gods. Blackboard and lecture-platform texts are taking over the set. Some of the numbers of that first disheartening concert of mine resembled nothing so much as greatly exaggerated oratorical gestures; today the performers are supplying the orations! Dullness upon dullness!! Who can but wonder why our dancer has to be letting the insipidities of her unimpressive brain come between the fountain-source of her genius and the marvel of that all-expressive body on which she has been laboring the better part of her life?

The plague of poems, editorials, and exclamations has been

FIGURE 3. Martha Graham (United States, 1945)

furthered (ironically enough) by the one great creative development within the field—the "dance play," namely, of Miss
Martha Graham. This wondrous genre has rules, qualities, and
a horizon of its own, which, strictly speaking, are of the timeless realm of dream, rather than of the heart-rhythm of the
jungle of life. Dance enters into these surrealistic conjurations
to be experienced not directly, but so to speak, in profoundest
retrospect. The magic lies in the atmosphere of incorporeal
unsubstantiality; the actual dance performances of the characters involved are astonishingly slight. Poem-fragments, dance-
fragments, scenery-fragments, music-fragments, charged with a
continuous hypnotic spell, phosphoresce in a sleep landscape,
where mysteriously motivated personages come and go. Clearly
this rich art is not a direct development out of the primary
technique-discoveries of the Modern Dance, but a fresh creation
out of the soul of a great Modern Dancer. It is a whole new

category. To seek from it an answer to my distracted question of the technique demonstration would be to deny its peculiar excellence and wonder.

Meanwhile, unhappily, the entire Modern Movement is going over to little plays and to a horrendous bastard-art of poem-dancing. Unmitigated dance has died the death. Let me utter the whole complaint in the words of the Gracehoper to the Ondt in James Joyce's *Finnegans Wake*:

> Your genus its worldwide, your spacest sublime!
> But, Holy Saltmartin, why can't you beat time?[2]

Asking for a beat instead of a text I may be off the beam. Nevertheless, I cannot but feel that it would be something of an experience to watch, for an evening, a dancer with faith enough in her body's craft to let the book salesmen go hang.

Has anyone else been suffering from this feeling?

Text, or Idea? (1944)[1]

Since Mr. Beiswanger[2] has honored my first effort to state the case for the "presentational" as against the "discoursive" principle in art—but specifically in the dance—by pointing out that the problem was hardly broached by my rhapsodic flier, I feel encouraged to attempt a brief series of clarifications. In my first essay, "Betwixt the Cup and the Lip" (the present paper is, so to say, a napkin to the chin), I described—if overecstatically!—my personal responses to a technique demonstration. The point I wished to make was that when the Modern Dancer is not troubled by serious "arty" or didactic intentions, then even the simplest elements of her craft carry a "presentational" power that has remained (at least so far as my experience is concerned) unexploited on the concert stage. The reason for the fiasco seems to be that, instead of developing the "presentational" elements of the craft in terms of a "presentational" logic, the Modern Dancer is being wrong-headedly advised to invoke a nonaesthetic, even anti-aesthetic principle to effect the work of amplification and coordination—namely, a "discoursive," didactic, intellectualistic, nonvisual, nonjoyous principle: the principle of Herr Professor at the Blackboard and Mr. Senator on the Stump. I did not wish to suggest that dance should be mere technique, or that formal disorganization should pass for a profoundly conceived and skillfully rendered production. My point was rather that a basic misconception of the ends of art is persistently intervening to botch the work of our young creators—briefly, the notion that a literary thesis is a creative idea.

Mind must not be identified with Brain, nor Ideas with Thoughts and Words. Mind includes the senses, the feelings, and the faculty of intuition, as well as the mental department housed under the skull. Hence a Creative Idea (an idea that touches and moves the Mind) is not a thought culled from a text, but a realization derived from full experience, and precisely, a realization of some form-giving principle. Such a realization can present itself through a sense-perception, or by a disposition of the feelings, or in a moment of intuitive insight, as well as—or even better than—through a conclusion arrived at by the brain.

FIGURE 4. Anna Duncan (United States, 1921)

In general, it can be expected that the inspiration of the dancer will derive from nonverbal sources. She is no virtuoso of the cerebrum. Of all people, she is the least constrained to conception through the head. But if, by chance, some word, some phrase or sentence from a book, should move her imagination, then she must retire to her own quietness and brood the mysterious gift. The seed requires time to stir to life the contents of her own silence. She is to body forth a materialization, not a charade.

The dancer, that is to say, is not a semaphorist, but a work of art in the flesh; her function is not to flash messages back and forth from brain to brain (that is the role of the discursive paragraph), but to embody Significant Form. And what is Significant Form? It is the rhythm of life projected in design; the invisible pattern of the psyche reflected in time and space; a profoundly inspired disposition of feeling-charged materials stemming from, and addressed to, that creative center where human consciousness and the unconscious fruitfully touch.

The first slip, then, betwixt the cup and the lip, my earlier article diagnosed as the fault of a wrong notion concerning the nature of the Creative Idea: the elements of dance are composed according to a mistaken principle and forfeit, as a result, their value. The second slip was described as a failure to find the distinction between the logic of dance and that of drama.

Now, the minute a dancer introduces into her composition a personality characterization, a narrative element, a touch of satire, or a poetical phrase, she enters, more or less, into the literary field and becomes subject to the laws of that empire. The audience automatically falls into patterns of literary experience and expectation. Consequently, unless the artist knows what she is doing and knows also how to manipulate dramatic-literary materials, she runs the risk of producing, instead of tragic terror and pity only bathos, and instead of comic joy only burlesque jocularity.

This is not to say that the dance-play should not or cannot

exist. Indeed it does exist, has existed for millenniums, and will exist, no doubt, as long as human beings permit themselves to experience and create. The point is rather that a distinction must be made between the formal principles of the two arts—dance and dance-drama—if either is to prosper.

A third slip, and the one that seemed to me to typify the whole series, is that of composing parallel to poetry or even to clippings from the newspaper. The problem of dance-logic here is reneged; the art is reduced to pantomime and expanded oratorical gesture. Moreover, if there should be, by happy chance, a moment of effective dance, the power of it would be short-circuited by text. For words and phrases are risky things for any artist to handle—largely because in everyday life they are employed in practical, discursive communication. The great effort, for example, of the poet is to make his verbal materials point past or through their immediate connotations to the depth-world of the soul, and this he does by rhythmic composition, repetition of refrain, sounding of overtone and undertone, emphasis on consonant or on vowel.... The risk is always that the literal, easy, matter-of-fact reference of everyday communication may blind the eye to the finally ineffable idea which the poet is concerned to realize. And now, if the idea is really rendered in the poem, there it is! Why dance a dance to it? If the idea is not there rendered, why bring forward the poem at all? But if it is thought that a wedding of word and gesture can be achieved, then we must study as painstakingly our rhetoric as our choreography. We may think we have mastered the art of words and phrases because we know how to order lamb chops in a restaurant and to read the columns of the daily press. But when it comes to giving verbal expression to the living silences of the heart, few can do better than stutter: still fewer can achieve anything worth a ticket costing fifty cents!

The mistake of mistakes is the apparently plausible notion that to say something one has to say something. But what the artist has to present is wordless. Art brings out and presents to

the mind the living structure-lines of the cosmos: this presentation reveals to us the proportions of our being: this revelation
sets our minds in harmony for a moment: and this harmony is
the bath of life. That is why the artist is exorbitantly praised.
The artist is the magician of re-creation. But if now it is journalism, sociology, patriotism, bathos, clownery, and amateur theatrics we are to be fed—well then, let us come well bibbed and
aproned, and prepared for every kind of nursery accident. After
all, we have only to put ourselves in the right frame of mind, and
anything can be fun.

The Jubilee of Content and Form (1945)[1]

NIETZSCHE DECLARES SOMEWHERE that for the true artist "form *is* the content of a work of art." Though the layman normally is interested only in the subject matter and looks *through* the traits of form without even noting them—almost as if through a pane of glass—form for the artist must be the paramount concern. A still life by Monet is a very different thing from one by Picasso, not because of the subject matter (which in the case of a still life is obviously of an indifferent, neutral order), but because of contrasting qualities of form. From the artist's standpoint therefore, any purchaser who has no feeling for these qualities but only a requirement for bright flowers on the wall is a calamity. The tragedy of the artist in the modern world might be summed up by an estimate of the probability of this calamity befalling any given production of his creative mine.

But on the other hand, there is something to be said for the common propensity of the layman. Subject matter actually makes an ineradicable contribution even to the most abstract, least "literary" work of art. An evening with Sigmund Freud and the *Pedagogical Sketchbook* of Paul Klee will suffice to open the eye to the insidious communicative powers, for example, even of such apparently innocent forms as circles, dots, straight and wavy lines. Two apples of Cézanne, one of them cut and opened

FIGURE 5. Untitled drawing by Paul Klee (watercolor and pencil on paper, Germany, c. 1914)

by a knife—and we have before us (or at least our unconscious has before it) as lively a little human comedy as might be found in any French triangle. What then if we should shift our incorrigibly libidinous eye from such essentially chaste, inhuman art materials as canvasses and paint to the vivid palette of leaping male and female figures, which is the theater of the dance? Form or no form, nature will work on us its vulgar will!

And so I beg to approach without further ado the lay-minded problem of Subject Matter in the Dance—not the entire problem, indeed, for this is a magnitudinous affair, but a single, not too complicated aspect, namely the problem of mythological material in the dance: the materials of myth, legend, fairytale, and fable. The dance, like all the arts, came into being in a rich, primeval atmosphere of mythological inspiration, long served society as a conjuring instrument, and matured in a context of godly and demonic presences. The dissolution of that context, as a result of the development of the modern, scientifically grounded disbelief in supernatural agencies, left the dance without its original metaphysical support. This was a crisis that affected all the arts. In reaction, there took place a general transfer of interest and attention from the supernatural to the natural scene. And the great problem of the artist became that of coping significantly with the materials of the world of common day.

FIGURE 6. "Greek" dancers (United States, c. 1920)

Meanwhile, however, a nostalgic, comparatively trivial interest in the outmoded mythological materials remained to trouble the gradually maturing modern consciousness. The ancient world of gods and demons offered a mirage-like yet gratifying sanctuary to the more delicate spirits among us who, for one reason or another, chose to refuse the challenge of the world of waking-consciousness. Myth, legend, fairytale, and fable, compounded with airy wisps and foams from the half-forbidden worlds of erotic dream, gracefully treated in a manner Aubrey Beardsleyish, or else hocus-pocusly thumped about to the tune of anthropological chit-chat ("imitative magic" and "the fertility of the soil"), persistently intruded into the modern laboratories of art. And the modern spirit permitted itself, in its lighter moments, to take delight in these airy nothings—for the sake (of course) of the aesthetic, stylistic achievements of the master craftsmen who had endowed them with Significant

Form. Like the flowers and lemons of a still life, the nymphs and fauns, totem presences and sacrificial maidens supplied a harmless, not unattractive base for breathtaking virtuoso deeds of sheerest, highest art: pirouettes, entrechats, contractions, and releases, runs and falls.

But now let us open the instructive work of Dr. Freud: *The Interpretation of Dreams* (1900), and the still more instructive opus of Dr. C. G. Jung: *Psychology of the Unconscious* (1912); after that, let us glance at the six volumes of Dr. Stith Thompson's *Motif-Index of Folk-Literature* (1932–36); and finally, let us turn again to the inspired pages of the Symbolists and Romantics of the nineteenth century. What do we learn? Well, we learn that over the entire inhabited world, in spite of many colorful and distracting variations of nomenclature and costumes, the episodes and personages of myth, legend, fairytale, and fable remain, and have remained throughout all time, essentially the same. Also we learn that these mysteriously constant personages and episodes are precisely those that have been upsetting or delighting us in our personal fantasies and dreams. Oedipus and Orestes, the Sun Bird and the Serpent are known not only to the scholar's study but also to the lunatic asylum and the nightly pillow. Mythology, in other words, is not an outmoded quaintness of the past, but a living complex of archetypal, dynamic images, native to, and eloquent of, some constant, fundamental stratum of the human psyche. And that stratum is the source of the vital energies of our being. Out of it proceed all the fate-creating drives and fears of our lives. While our educated, modern waking-consciousness has been going forward on the wheels and wings of progress, this recalcitrant, dream-creating, wish-creating, under-consciousness has been holding to its primeval companions all the time, the demons and the gods.

Apparently, then, the archetypal figures of myth undercut the rational interests of our conscious life, and touch directly the vital centers of the unconscious. The artist who knew how to manipulate these archetypes would be able to conjure with the energies of the human soul. For the symbols are as potent as they ever were. The artist who really knew their secrets might still play the magician—the priest of the potent sign—working marvels purging the community of its pestilential devils and bringing purity and peace. Only, we should tend to explain his effects in psychological rather than theological terms: the heavens and hells being now reinterpreted as chambers of the unconscious. And we should revere him no less than he was revered in the days of yore, when his poems conjured thunderheads and his dances moved the spirits of the soil.

It is safe to say that many of the greater men and women who have wrought in modern times with the images of myth have been conscious of the powers in their hands. They have regarded themselves, in a way, as priests and priestesses—and not without justification. Comparatively few, however, have seriously dedicated themselves to a thoroughgoing study of the laws and powers of the mythological archetypes. And this is a misfortune; for it is certain that a proper symbol authoritatively handled must inevitably touch, fascinate, and work its effects upon even the dullest human wit. Indeed, there is good reason to believe that what an audience really seeks when it approaches the altar of art is some operation of this kind. From the audience's standpoint therefore, any "genius" who has no authority over his symbols but only a talent for sensational arrangements is a fake. And the tragedy of the audience in the modern world might be summed up by an estimate of the probability of a pretty faker appearing behind the footlights, or a solemn one behind the traditional beard.

To resolve the hard dilemma a correspondence must be discovered between the psychological effects of aesthetic form and those of the archetypes of myth and symbol. Ideally, the two poles of attention—that of the artist, that of the layman—should be so coordinated as to become virtually identical. *Every aesthetic element holds a psychological value identical with the psychological value of some mythological element.* The task of the artist who chooses to handle mythological materials (and one can extend this by a fairly obvious calculation even to the artist who chooses the materials of the world of common day) is to grasp fully the implications of his images and then render them with the precisely appropriate elements of his craft. In this way, content is the *source* of form, the *mother* of form. Content, one might even dare to say, *is* form. Thus we have been brought full-circle from the snobbery of art-for-art: full-circle, where the mutually antagonistic extremes meet and fuse.

The Ancient
Hawaiian Hula (1946)[1]

THE HULAS OF ANCIENT HAWAII, like the traditional dances of the Orient, had nothing to do with the display of the personality or personal emotions of the dancer. They were not the creations of self-expressive artists, but revelations handed down, without change, from generation to generation. The dancer was the transmitter of a supra-personal, anonymous, inherited form, and literally a priestess. Her costume (like the robes of a king or the vestments of a priest) set her apart; converted her, for the moment of her dance, into a sacred image, a living icon, the visible, temporary manifestation of an immortal presence. She was therefore *tabu*, her dance *tabu*, and the place of her dance *tabu*.

FIGURE 7. Hula dancers (United States, c. 1901)

Tabu is a Polynesian word signifying "full of spiritual power," hence, "not to be touched." In contrast to *tabu* is the word and state of *noa*: the profane. When the world is experienced not as symbolic of eternal archetypes, but as a context of transitory, mortal things (that is to say, not a "super-nature," but as "nature"), it is *noa*. When, on the other hand, it is felt as eloquent of the invisible, it is *tabu*.

Traditional art everywhere is *tabu*. Traditional art is a theophany: a manifestation in visible or audible form of the operation of the Invisible and the Inaudible in nature, in society, and in the individual. Traditional art is a divine revelation, precisely as the Bible, for orthodox Jews, Christians, and Mohammedans, is a divine revelation. Among the so-called native races of the world, every art and handicraft—whether music, dancing, sculpture, and painting, or canoe-making, house-making, pot-making, fishing, hunting, and sewing—was an exposition of certain fundamental traditional ideas, and these ideas were regarded as originally revealed to man by the gods themselves. The Hawaiians declare of their great dances, the great hulas: *no ke akua mai*. "They are from the gods." The beautiful and profoundly significant forms are believed to have come down from the *wa-po*, the Mythological Age at the beginnings of the world.

Now, mythology is not history (the rehearsal of literal fact), but vision (a pictorial symbolization of the backgrounds of existence). Hence the Mythological Age is regarded in Polynesia (as elsewhere) not merely as an era that once was, but also as a depth continually productive, lying just beneath and behind the surfaces of things. The Void, which in the beginning emitted the world, is continually, now and forever, creative of the forms that we behold. The Void, that is to say, is our own interior, the perpetual source. The Great Dances speak not only of the beginnings of the world, therefore, but of the depth within ourselves.

In Polynesia, where the problems symbolized in myth were studied profoundly, these depths (at once metaphysical and metapsychological) are described in a great number of extraordinarily impressive cosmogonic images. The following, from New Zealand, is a good example. Here the primal Void is represented as giving forth a series of gradually condensing states of emanation, which precipitate, finally, the bounding walls of Space:

> The Void
> The First Void
> The Second Void
> The Vast Void
> The Far-Extending Void
> The Sere Void
> The Unpossessing Void
> The Delightful Void
> The Void Fast Bound
> The Night
> The Hanging Night
> The Drifting Night
> The Moaning Night
> The Daughter of Troubled Sleep
> The Dawn
> The Abiding Day
> The Bright Day
> Space
> In Space two existences without shape were formed, a male existence and a female; and from these sprang Father Heaven and Mother Earth. Father Heaven and Mother Earth were the parents of the gods.

Mythologies everywhere personify the power of creation as "God": the Supreme Creator, maker of the world, mankind, and the gods (or angels). In the Hebrew mythology this highest role is assigned to the tribal divinity Yahweh, or Jehovah: he is the local personification of the unknowable Unknown. Comparably, in the cosmogonic myths of Polynesia the sea-god Taaroa fills this role. The following is a Society Islands version of his work of creation:

> He existed. Taaroa was his name.
> In the immensity
> There was no earth, there was no sky,
> There was no sea, there was no man.

Taaroa calls, but nothing answers.
Existing alone, he became the universe.
Taaroa is the root, the rocks.
Taaroa is the sands.
It is thus that he is named.
Taaroa is the light.
Taaroa is within.
Taaroa is the germ.
Taaroa is the support.
Taaroa is enduring.
Taaroa is wise.
He erected the land of Hawaii,
Hawaii the great, the sacred,
As a body or shell for Taaroa.
The earth is moving.
O Foundations, O Rocks, O Sands,
Hither, hither,
Brought hither, pressed together the earth.
Press, press again.
They do not unite.
Stretch out the seven heavens, let ignorance cease.
Create the heavens, let darkness cease.
Let immobility cease.
Let the period of messengers cease.
It is the time of the speaker.
Completed the foundations,
Completed the rocks,
Completed the sands,
The heavens are enclosing,
The heavens are raised.
In the depths is finished the land of Hawaii.

The various dances and chants of the Hawaiians are graded
in sanctity according to the profundities they reveal. The most
holy are those treating of the gods and kings; for it is through
the symbolic presences of the invisible god and visible kings that
the powers sustaining creation are made manifest to human
consciousness. The gods and kings are the highest conceivable
symbols of the Unconceivable. The chants and hulas treating of
them are either unaccompanied, or else supported by the impressive and eloquent resonances of the drums (*pahu*), the deep

organ-tones of great bamboo cylinders thumped against the ground (*ka-eke-eke*), or the boom of pounding calabashes (*ipu*). In a presentation of hulas these noble and extremely solemn dances would always appear in the first portion of the program.

The second portion was devoted to themes of a lesser order, though still *tabu*. Melodies and dances of this rank could be accompanied by lesser instruments: pebble-castanets (*ili-ili*), rattles (*uli-uli*), little staffs of frayed bamboo (*puili*), or wooden batons struck against each other (*kala-au*). The songs (or *meles*) are commonly pleasant little poems of love and nature, treating of common human beings and of the beautiful valleys and beaches and pleasant villages that they inhabit. But always (here, just as in the more solemn *meles*), by subtle and delicate allegorical devices, the play of the divine powers into our world of common day is continually insisted upon.

The final dances of the traditional hula program were of an order which it is a little difficult for the modern Western spirit to appreciate in the proper way. They were frankly sexual and comical: but again, with the understanding that divine potencies are here in play. And just as the first dances were often in celebration of the great Kings and Queens, so these were in jubilant celebration of the genitals of the Kings and Queens—which were given personal nicknames and then treated as independently adventuring entities. Songs of this kind (at once hilarious and religious) are as old as human civilization: they belong to the mood of Mardi Gras—and are not for Puritans.

The King or Headman of the district was the promoter and supporter of the hula. At his court were gathered the bards and men of lore (skilled in mythology, tradition, genealogy, proverbial wisdom), and also the members of the younger set, the sons and daughters of the noble families together with their handsome friends. The leader and organizer of the company was the Kumu, or "Priest of the Hula"—a position open only to one who had properly fitted himself by training and study. The Kumu might be called to his position by the choice of some young people who wished to form a company, or he might be a skilled dancer who wished to organize a company himself; or again, he might be appointed by the King or Headman, to train a group for state occasions.

The hula hall or school precinct (*Halau*) was regarded as a temple: a temple to Laka, the goddess-patroness of the hula, who was called "The Fount of Joy" and "The One Whose Presence Gives Life." She was a benign divinity, a goddess of flowers, and one of the gentler modes or manifestations of the Mother of the World. In one of the prayers to her she is besought to come and take possession of the dancer, her devotee, to dwell in him as in a temple, to inspire all his parts and faculties, and to guide his voice, hands, body, and feet. Her sister, Pele, goddess of the terrific fire-and-lava fury of the volcano, represented the dangerous, annihilating aspect of the same great cosmic principle. Pele figures prominently in the hub traditions of the islands.

Within the hula hall stood an altar (*Kuahu*) dedicated to the goddess. This was Laka's visible abode. Her presence was symbolized by a rude block of uncarved wood arrayed in yellow tapa cloth and scented with turmeric. The altar was decorated with abundant offerings of flowers, *maile, ie-ie, hala-pepe, lehua,* ginger blossoms, etc., and was delightful with the sweetness of tropical scents.

Life within the *Halau* was *tabu*. Observances of fasts and other abstinences were insisted upon. There was a door guardian to supervise the threshold and permit only those to enter who could give the password (usually a fragment from some *mele* or hula chant). He sprinkled the entering person with holy water (seawater mixed with turmeric), and this indicated symbolically the transit from the realm of *noa* into that of *tabu*. Within the little temple was a staff of special cooks, servants, fishermen, and other helpers, who took care of the company during their session and made it possible for them to exist in total seclusion from the secular world.

Symbolism and the Dance, Part 1 (1950)[1]

THE WORD *symbol* is based on a Greek verbal root *bal*, meaning "to throw," to which is added the prefix *sym*, "together." *Symballein*, the verb, means, therefore, "to throw or bring together, to unite"; and so our English noun, "symbol," refers primarily to a sign or token that brings two things, or brings a number of things, together.

A merchant, for example, in ancient Greece, who bought a shipment of oil, wine, or olives, received, as a kind of invoice, a broken piece of bone, the other half of which was then attached to his order. When the goods arrived in port, or at the warehouse, he showed his claim to them by presenting his piece of bone, which fitted precisely into the half attached to the crate. Such tokens were known, specifically, as symbols—and though this word, during the centuries since, has been applied to many different spheres of human experience, it still carries with it some sense of its original reference. A true symbol is always a token that restores, one way or another, some kind of broken unit.[2]

Perhaps the best-known counterpart, in modern American life, of the symbol of the Greek merchant is the Chinese laundry ticket that we receive when we bring our shirts in to be washed. It is obvious how this works. There is a bit of Chinese writing on the ticket and this is torn in half—or else there is a number,

27

which is printed twice. The end of the week we return, and after a wait (sometimes of considerable suspense), while laundryman goes along with our portion of the ticket matching it to all the other half tickets on the dozens of piled-up bundles, the desired object is found, and we experience a peaceful feeling of satisfaction. The principal thing, of course, in this operation is not the ticket but the shirt. We should feel cheated if we received only the other half of our ticket, or if someone else's shirt had been slipped into our bundle, or if the shirt returned were ruined—faded out or torn (which later cheat, unfortunately, is nowadays, at least in Manhattan, part of the game). The symbol is only a means to an end. In general (or at least in the good old days, before "Chinese Hand Laundry" meant Hoboken Chemical Vat and Mangle), you would find your own dear shirt in the bundle, and it would fit when you put it on—and so you would be blessed, for a moment, with an earthly particle of that timeless delight which is the portion of the souls of the just in Paradise: the beatitude of the right man in the right place.

Thus the reunion of the halves of the ticket is a means to an end, not the end in itself; and so it might appropriately be asked whether the reunion of the man with his shirt may not, perhaps, be symbolic, too. For example, if the shirt cost him a lot of money, its return represents a reunion of the man with his own substance. Or the shirt may have been purchased, say, at Waikiki, and when the gentleman puts it on it gives him a sense of reunion with the casual, romantic old beach-boy that he was out there among the palms and ukuleles. Or again, the shirt may have been given to him by some beautiful woman; let us say, his wife. In all these cases, the man and his shirt can be regarded as the two halves of a symbol.

And so now we can press this inquiry one step further; we can ask: May not this man and his wife be the halves of a symbol, too? Plato in the *Symposium* recounts a curious myth devoted to this theme.

Man and woman, Plato tells us, were a single being, originally. "This primeval being was round, its back and sides forming a circle; and it had four hands and four feet, one head but two faces, looking opposite ways, set on a round neck and precisely alike; also four ears, and the remainder to correspond. It could walk upright as men do now, backward or forward as it pleased, and it could also roll over at a great pace, turning on its four hands and four feet, eight in all, like tumblers going over and over with their legs in the air; this was when it wanted to run fast...." Terrible was the might and strength of these early beings, Plato tells us, and they made an attack upon the gods. But the gods defeated them and split them in half, to reduce their strength. Then the halves were separated from each other. "And so each of us," we read, "thus separated, having one side only, like a flat fish, is but the indenture of a man, and is always looking for his other half."

A comparable image appears in the Bṛhadāraṇyaka Upaniṣad, which is an ancient Hindu text of about the seventh century B.C. and thus some three centuries earlier than Plato. "In the beginning this whole universe," we are told there, "was but the Self in human form....He was not at all happy; therefore people are still unhappy when alone. He desired a mate. He became as big as a man and wife embracing. Then he separated that great body in two. That is why this body that we have is only half of us, like one of the two halves of a split pea."

Or once again: we all have heard of the wonderful event in the Garden of Eden, when the Producer (as James Joyce phrases it) "caused a deep abuliousness to descend upon the Father of Truants and, at a side issue, pluterpromptly, brought on the scene the cutletsized consort."[3] According to the mystical teaching of the Hebrew Kabbalah, every couple is transcendentally one—just as Adam and Eve were one before the momentous tearing in half of the human totality in the Garden. Moreover, people who are virtuous find their proper half, but those who allow themselves to be distracted by the deceits of the senses bring home the wrong bundle from the laundry—and their fate, then, is like that of wearing someone else's shirt for life.

True lovers know instinctively that they are one; and they dwell, consequently, in that atmosphere of timeless delight which is the air of Paradise. They take great joy in exchanging tokens; and these lovers' tokens are real symbols, in the primary sense of the word. It is said that, long ago, one lover would wear one earring and the other the other—thus restoring, in a way, the broken unit. In these terms, one might say that the mighty jolt, which is the recognition of love, is nothing more or less than the sudden recognition that one is but a fraction, and that the completing fraction has been found.

FIGURE 8. Dancers (United States, 1939)

In the dance this mystery is symbolized in the popular couple dance. One can see that there are two, but also that they are one. Moreover, the dancing makes it clear that the feeling proper to this united state is timeless joy. The weight of the earth has been left below. Time and space, economics and politics, have dropped away. Like a double-headed angel soaring in the clouds, or more often, like a pair of elephants gamboling in the clearing of a jungle, the wondrous dual being moves timelessly to music. There is no need to rehearse the great variety of popular dances in which this poetical living image presents itself throughout the world. Its meaning—the basic one of all great symbols—is *the conjunction of opposites*: the reunion of the halves that transcendentally, primordially, ideally, or utopianly, are one—in this case, the two halves of that universal: Man.

FIGURE 9. "The World" (Italy, 1865)

Numerous symbols of the conjunction of opposites will be found in the mythological traditions of the world. The most obvious, perhaps, is that of the hermaphrodite, combining the attributes of the female and male. Among the numbered picture cards of the gypsy Tarot pack, for example, is one (number XXI) which is named "The World" and shows a dancing hermaphrodite. This carries down to modern times the figure of the universal Self that we found in the Bṛhadāraṇyaka Upaniṣad, Plato's *Symposium*, and the Book of Genesis. Likewise Tiresias, the mysterious, blind prophet who appears in Sophocles's *Oedipus Rex*, is supposed to have been both female and male. Moreover, many of the ancestral images of the Africans and Melanesians are represented as hermaphrodite: so also, the costumes representing the same beings in the festival dances of those peoples. Obviously, what is here symbolized is that transcendent totality from which all derives, which includes all things, and to which all beings return.

Another polarity commonly transcended in the symbols of mythology and legend is that of Age and Youth. The universal goddess, for example, is always both young and old, ever-living yet ageless, whether as Demeter, Isis, Ishtar, and Astarte, or as Parvati of India. H. Rider Haggard played upon this theme in his curious adventure novel *She*. Similarly, Merlin, in the Arthurian romances of the Middle Ages, can appear either as an old man or as a child. He combines the qualities of both, sometimes quickly alternating in his manifestations. And, of course, we find in many traditions the figure of the *Puer Aeternus*, or "Eternal Child" of miraculous powers: Jesus teaching in the Temple, Kṛṣṇa dancing among the Milkmaids, and Eros, the classical deity of love, who is at once the oldest and the youngest of gods.

One could go on citing instances forever. In the awesome form of the boon-bestowing serpent, for example, Good and Evil are combined, as they are also in the figure of God in the Book of Job. Kālī, the terrible goddess of India, is at once the Mother and Destroyer of the world, combining Life and Death. The Christian Crucifix unites the ideas of Death and Life in a single concept, as do also (though in a much less sublime way) such horripilating figures as Lazarus—and the Zombi. God as the Alpha and Omega, the Source and the Goal, is the fire to which all sparks return, the ocean to which all rivers flow and from which their waters, ultimately, were derived. Recognition-and-return is the great theme and meaning of the religious concept of Atonement, as well as of the various mythological romances of the hero's finding of his goddess-bride.[4] And in a humorous myth of the Gnostic tradition, the idea is rendered vividly by the glorious meeting of the soul, when it enters heaven, with its own radiant heaven-shirt, which it left behind when it descended to be born.

FIGURE 10. Śiva Naṭarāja (bronze, India, eleventh century)

The most complete and eloquent symbol of all, perhaps, is that of the dancing Lord of the World, the Hindu deity Śiva, as depicted in certain South Indian bronzes. Here the god's right foot is planted on a prostrate dwarf (whose name is Non-Knowing), while the left leg is lifted with the foot pointing toward the right. The first leg denotes the driving of souls into life and the second their release. The right hand, meanwhile, stretched out to the side, holds a little drum, the rhythm of which is time, the first principle of creation; but on the left palm, balancing opposite, is a flame, denoting the destruction of the world. Another right hand, however, is lifted palm forward, in the gesture meaning "Fear not!" while a second left hand is carried out before the body, pointing downward, calling attention to the lifted foot—that is to say, to the promise of release. This great god, who is the Creator, Preserver, and Destroyer of the world, wears a woman's earring in his left ear and a man's in his right; in his wildly flying hair are both the crescent-moon of growing life and the skull of death. The mysteriously unsmiling, mask-like head of the god, in spite of the dynamism of the rest of his image, is absolutely still—poised in eternity. This corresponds to that immovable point of stillness within, which the dancer knows, which the artist knows, out of which all creation springs and all courage to live.

The dancing god is here a symbol of the union of time and eternity, the spontaneity of eternity in time. The same idea is expressed in the whirling dances, culminating in ecstasy, of certain sects of dervishes, and likewise in a curious version of the Last Supper, rendered in the apocryphal Acts of St. John, where the twelve apostles revolve in a dance around Jesus, like the twelve constellations of the Zodiac going around the sun. We are reminded of this apocryphal Paschal mystery when we read that in a number of the French cathedrals, during the Middle Ages, the bishop and his clergy used to dance together on Easter eve, and when we are told of the Hassidic dances in the seventeenth-century ghettos. In these latter, the polarity of life's misery and the beatitude of eternity was transcended, by virtue of a simple, vital faith in the ubiquity of God in his created world.

Here, then, is dance both as an aid to the discovery of the creative point and as a manifestation pouring forth from it: dance as Yoga and dance as Revelation. This dual function is of the essence of every living symbol, every living religion, every living art. Moreover, such a symbol is not merely a means, but in a sense an end: the highest possible vehicle of man's timeless joy in the dialectic of his transcendence and experience of the pairs of opposites. "The dancer," writes Plotinus (*Ennead* 3.2.16) "is an image of Life."

(To be continued.)

Symbolism and the Dance, Part 2 (1950)[1]

THE POWER OF A SYMBOL to unite not merely two persons, things, or principles, but many, is illustrated in the dances of the Andaman Islands. The Negrito pygmies of the large but inaccessible archipelago some 350 miles off the Burma coast are counted among the most primitive races on earth. When discovered they could not produce fire artificially, though they hunted

FIGURE 11. Andaman islanders (Myanmar, c. 1906–8)

wild pig with beautiful long bows and cooked the meat (as well as fish, sea turtle, and dugong) over carefully cherished flames. They possessed small outrigger canoes, but never ventured from their islands, where they must have been marooned for thousands of years. They made use of stone only for shaving and scarifying the skin, all their other implements being of shell, bone, and wood. And they dwelt in tiny communities of not more than forty or fifty souls: mere circles of eight or nine family huts standing around an elliptical central area, which was cleared, every night, to serve as a dancing ground. For these little people, we are told, were indefatigable dancers.

Professor Radcliffe-Brown, who visited them in the years 1906–8, describes their typical evening in the following terms:[2] "When all is ready a man who has volunteered to sing the first song takes his stand at the sounding-board [which is a great hardwood slab fixed in the ground at an angle, at one end of the dancing area], and sings his song through. When he reaches the chorus, the women [who are seated in a row behind the sounding-board, with their legs stretched out in front of them] take up the chorus and repeat it after him, and as they do so each woman marks time by clapping her hands on the hollow formed by her thighs, the legs being crossed one over the other at the ankle. The singer continues to sing, thus leading the chorus, and at the same time marks the time of the song by beating on the sounding-board with his foot. As soon as the chorus begins the dancers begin to dance. The step of each dancer is the same, but there is very little attempt to form a figure. When the singer and the chorus get tired, the singing ceases, but the man at the sounding-board continues to mark time for the dancers. The singer repeats his song several times, and he may sing several songs, each repeated several times. When he gets tired he is relieved by another man. In a dance that lasts for any time, one singer succeeds another, and the singing and dancing are kept up continuously, sometimes for five or six hours."

FIGURE 12. Andaman islanders, peace-making dance (Myanmar, c. 1906–8)

"In the dance of the Southern tribes," our observer continues, "each dancer dances alternately on the right foot or on the
left. When dancing on the right foot the first movement is a
slight hop with the right foot, then the left foot is raised and
brought down with a backward scrape along the ground, then
another hop on the right foot. These three movements, which
occupy the time of two beats of the song, are repeated until the
right leg is tired, and the dancer then changes the movement
to a hop with the left foot, followed by a scrape with the right
and another hop with the left.... The body of the dancer is bent
forward slightly from the hips, the legs being flexed at the knees
and the back being curved well inwards. There are several ways
of holding the hands and arms, one of the commonest being to
hold the arms outstretched in front on a level with the shoulders,
while the thumb and forefinger of one hand are interlocked with
those of the other.... As a man dances he remains in one spot

for a short time, and then, still continuing the same step, moves for a yard or two around the circle of the dancing ground. Every now and then a dancer is to be seen trotting from one position to another across the dancing ground, abandoning the step of the dance, but still keeping time to the song."

An uncomplicated, monotonous, and (one would think) infinitely dull affair, yet these curious little Andamanese have been at it every night for literally thousands of years. Moreover, as Dr. Franz Boas tells us,[3] the members of small and isolated primitive communities of this kind resemble each other as closely as the members of a single family; for they all inherit the same stock of genes, all having precisely the same ancestors. And so we must imagine an extraordinarily homogeneous little company, everybody looking almost exactly like everybody else, going round and round in their minute village compound by firelight—for centuries—simply fascinated with themselves.

The spell of this primitive dance derives from the fact that it is a uniting symbol, joining not merely two apparently separate beings, but forty or fifty: the members of a community. Quarrels, jealousies, and the normal daily frictions develop as well among the Andamanese as in any Christian home; and yet, when these people assemble on their dancing ground and are united (or rather reunited) by a single pulse, they function as a unit—which is what they really are. The dancing area itself is a kind of temenos, or sacred area, in which a heightened sense of communal solidarity is experienced; as though a magic circle had been drawn shutting out the common-day reality of separate individuals and facilitating the experience of the other reality—that of their identity; for these villagers *are*, in essence, one. Each owes the genes that formed him, the techniques by which he lives, the words with which he thinks, and the ideas that he entertains, to this social group: his life is but a moment of its larger life. And since there is something really wondrous about the realization of this other, more intrinsic reality, which is so different from the more obvious one of individual separateness, the dance, or symbol that reveals it, is an inexhaustible delight.

The Andamanese have other symbols, also, communicating the same realization, and these are the coordinating supports of the community: rites of birth, adolescence, marriage, burial, war, peace, etc. Both in these and in the nightly dances, decoration plays an important role. White clay, red paint, pandanus leaves, and shell fringes transform and sublimate the human body into a supernormal, really wondrous form—man's festival form—in respect to which there is a peculiar spirit of make-believe, coupled with an intense, deeply joyous seriousness, which is typical of the mood of ritual and myth throughout the world.

The Negrito pygmies, in their uncomplicated, tiny, and homogeneous communities, require little to let them realize their intrinsic identity with each other; hence their symbolic system is only rudimentary. The case becomes more complex in a highly differentiated society. The arts and rites then become much more elaborate, the festivals much more impressive—and, proportionately, much more important, much less playful, much more intense. But before considering this greatly complicated aspect of our problem, I should like to call attention to one more idyllic scene.

The setting is West Africa and the period that of the First World War. The characters are Dr. Köhler's collection of pet chimpanzees who (or at least in the realm of Gestalt psychology) are no less famous today than Sir Isaac Newton's apple.

Two of the primates, Tschego and Grande, began to play at spinning around and around, and the other chimps soon picked up on it. Writes Köhler, "Any game of two together was apt to turn into this 'spinning top' play, which appeared to express a climax of friendly and amicable *joie de vivre*. The resemblance to a human dance became truly striking when the rotations were rapid, or when Tschego, for instance, stretched her arms out horizontally as she spun around. Tschego and Chica—whose favorite fashion during 1916 was this 'spinning'—sometimes combined a forward movement with the rotations, and so they revolved slowly round their own axes and along the playground.

"The whole *group* of chimpanzees sometimes combined in more elaborate *motion patterns.*[5] For instance, two would wrestle and tumble near a post; soon their movements would become more regular and tend to describe a circle round the post as a center. One after another, the rest of the group approach, join the two, and finally march in an orderly fashion round and round the post. The character of their movements changes; they no longer walk, they trot, and as a rule with special emphasis on one foot, while the other steps lightly; thus a rough approximate rhythm develops, and they tend to 'keep time' with one another....It seems to me extraordinary," concludes Dr. Köhler, "that there should arise quite spontaneously, among chimpanzees, anything that so strongly suggests the dancing of some primitive tribes."

One cannot fail to note the resemblance of this group trot, with its emphasis on one foot, to the nightly dance of the Andamanese. Moreover, the circumambulation of a post resembles the traditional round dance about a central figure (for example, that of the twelve apostles around Jesus, which was mentioned in our article of last month), while the whirling dance suggests—as Dr. Köhler has noted—the dervish dance of spiritual ecstasy.[6] Obviously, the basic feeling values of such motion patterns antecede the conceptual associations later attributed to them in human society. This, I believe, is one of the fundamental traits and mysteries of the symbol.

Indeed, the games of Dr. Köhler's chimpanzees point up the fact that the enigma of play, which is very close to that of art, must be studied, in its beginnings, among the higher animals— those whose young enjoy an extended period of parental protection: bear cubs, puppies and kittens, lion cubs, monkeys, the higher apes, etc. What such a period of parental protection does is to create a sphere in which the economic and political laws of the struggle for existence are suspended: the little animals' appetites have been satisfied, and there is nothing for them to fear. Immediately, there become manifest both the random acts and the regular motion patterns of a spontaneous exuberance. As in the dance of the Andamans, the temenos or protected area allows life to bubble, to act directly out of its own center, freed from the necessity of reacting to external pressures, and the result is virtually a transformation of nature. The laws of the jungle are temporarily in abeyance and we hear, as it were, the prelude to the song of man.

Animal exuberance, this mystery of play, is very close to (if not identical with) the basic impulse of genius in the arts. The power of great art to purge us—to release us, for a moment, from the jungle-melancholy of hungering, frightened, or drearily bored mankind—derives from its transcendence of the usual biological emotions. Released from fear and appetite, and fascinated by a game, we lose our egocentric emphasis and discover, suddenly, with an emotion of joy, that we can participate, in a spirit of free and charming geniality, with others—neither on their terms nor on our own, but in terms of a new and disinterested harmonization. Moreover, just as this delicious spirit of play is what is most human in the animals, so is it precisely what is most godlike in man. That is the meaning of the Indian image of the Cosmic Dancer. Śiva does not create the world because of any hunger on his part, or any fear—any economic or political necessity—but in divine spontaneity: the universe, with all its beings, is the shimmer of his dancing limbs. And each of us is Śiva in so far as he can live life as a dance. Or, as the poet-philosopher Nietzsche states it (*Thus Spake Zarathustra* 73.17–19): "His step betrayeth whether a person already walketh on *his own* path: just see me walk! He, however, who cometh nigh to his goal, danceth, —And though there be on earth fens and dense afflictions, he who hath light feet runneth even across the mud, and danceth, as upon wellswept ice."

(To be continued.)

Symbolism and the Dance, Part 3 (1950)[1]

NOW IT IS REALLY ASTOUNDING that Dr. Köhler's chimpanzees should have brought forth from their *joie de vivre* certain of the fundamental motion patterns of traditional human dances. This may mean, as I have suggested, that the primary sense of our most common expressive forms inheres in the animal level of the psyche and so antecedes whatever conceptual associations may be assigned to them by human beings. I name the ape dance at this point, however, not to develop a psychological theory, but because the little shock of recognizing our spiritual as well as physical affinity with the primates may help us to understand what the early hunting peoples felt about the animals. Man and the animal were the two halves of a broken unit. Put together again, they would constitute a symbol through which might be experienced something of the mystery of being. Hence, those animal masks that figure so prominently in the collections of ethnological museums! The idea of a Golden Age, when man and beast had not yet been differentiated—an age of semi-human, semi-animal Ancestors—is the most persistent trait of primitive mythologies throughout the world.[2]

We today find it difficult to comprehend the eloquence of those millenniums of masked dancers that lie behind us in the human past and whose mysteries survive, fragmentarily, in the

FIGURE 13. *Ojibwa Snowshoe Dance* by George Catlin (United States, 1835)

marginal regions of the world. To give an inkling of their meaning, let me cite the words of a Pawnee priest, concerning a detail
of one of the rituals of his tribe. He had drawn a circle with
his toe. "The circle," he replied, when questioned, "represents
a nest, and it is drawn with the toe because the eagle builds its
nest with its claws. Although we are imitating the bird making
its nest, there is another meaning to the action, we are thinking
of God making the world for the people to live in. If you go on
a high hill and look around, you will see the sky touching the
earth on every side, and within this circular enclosure the people
live. So the circles we have made not only are nests, but they
also represent the circle God has made for the dwelling place of
all the people. The circles also stand for the kinship group, the
clan, and the tribe."³

Here is a telling instance of the power of the symbol to unite
a great number of things by supporting, on a simple base, an
elaborate structure of consonant conceptual allegory. Also evident is that feeling for serious play which I mentioned in my last

article as typical of the mythological-ritualistic mood. But what I wish particularly to indicate is the cosmic image that has here been rendered through an unpretentious animal symbol. The same idea is fundamental to Plato's philosophy of education; for, as we read in the *Timaeus*:[4] "There is only one way in which one being can serve another, and this is by giving him his proper nourishment and motion. And the motions which are akin to the divine principle within us are the thoughts and revolutions of the universe." Indeed, this Platonic and Pawnee concept of an inward relationship between man and the universe was basic to every one of the ancient civilizations and is the key to their symbolism. It is the source, moreover, of their dignity and mysteriously eloquent beauty; for the whole texture of life in those traditional societies was organized as a kind of hierophantic dance, making manifest those thoughts and revolutions of the universe of which Plato speaks.

The city of Babylon, for example, was an imitation of the cosmos. Its prodigious defending walls represented the bounds of the world, in the four directions. The river Euphrates, cutting it in two, divided it into a heavenly half and an earthly, the sacred Ziggurat, or temple of the god, being the axial point of the first and the royal palace that of the second; while the broad central boulevard from east to west represented the golden road of the sun-god across the lapis-lazuli sky. The four moments of the year when the sun comes to the solstices and equinoxes (on approximately March 21, June 22, September 23, and December 22) were occasions for gorgeous processions of acrobats and dancers, clowns, sacred animals, dancing warriors, trumpeters, and thundering drummers, along the solar boulevard, followed slowly and tremendously by the great carnival float of the sun-god himself. And there, like wooden images, sat the king and queen, the god and his consort on earth, while around them the world that they illuminated danced and sang.[5]

Counterparts of these seasonal rites appear in every corner of the inhabited earth. And they are the sources of the dances that today are appearing on our stages under the rubric of the "eth-nologic" movement. During the centuries, the symbolic forms have been utilized and modified in many ways—in the rough peasant games and dances of popular feasts as well as in the so-phisticated elegancies of court theatricals. Often, however, as in our own sentimental art of the ballet (in such a work as *Swan Lake*, for example), the earlier purport has been forgotten. And yet the magic of such inane decoctions—their perennial fascina-tion—may well derive from the dim echo within them of an ancient symbol.

What it meant to be a symbolic personage in one of those ancient, heavenly societies in the early period of our common human civilization can be gathered from a reading of Frazer's *Golden Bough.* At certain stated intervals (for example, when the moon and the planet Venus set together), the king was solemnly killed, or solemnly killed himself. Moreover, in some societies the king's entire court went with him, willingly, into a vast sub-terranean tomb: lords and ladies, musicians, dancers, officers of the guard, charioteers, and the royal stable. The girl harpist in the tomb of Queen Shu'ab of the ancient city of Ur was found with her fingers still touching the strings of her instrument; while the numerous entourage of the king (who had died some years before) stood in ordered ranks, deep underground.[6] Imag-ine the pageantry of such a burial: the solemn procession of the whole court of the moon-king down the ramp into the ground, to mark the end of an eon!

This seems to us insane. Nevertheless, it is the kind of act by which mankind transcended the simple laws of economics and created a civilization superior to the interests of mere biology. The mask, the costume, and the living of the role through to the end: by this device man detached himself from his personal pains and joys—just as a dancer does in a dance. Human life was literally sublimated, and man's body became, as it were, the vehicle of a god; that is to say, a symbol of the play of eternity in time. No matter what we today may think of this as a mode of life for rational beings, it is from the ages when life was lived this way that we inherit the very idea of art.

However—the whole spirit of the ancient symbols now is lost to us. We no longer sense the supporting presence of the animal ancestors; we no longer live the cosmic drama of the heavens. In fact, ever since the centuries of the Renaissance and Enlightenment, we have been boldly cutting ourselves off, quite intentionally, in every department of life and thought from the world of ritual, myth, and solemn fantasy. This is something to remember when trying to understand any masterpiece of traditional art—whether primitive, archaic, oriental, folk, or medieval; likewise, when watching an "ethnic" dance on the modern stage. Such a work is (for us) like a Buddhahead on a mantelpiece—or like the high hat in *Peter Pan* that was made to serve as a chimney. There is no relationship whatsoever between the object's original and present uses. Or it is like a fractured phrase lifted out of context to prove some completely irrelevant point.

Let us compare, for example, a few of the fundamental differences that distinguish the traditional from the modern work of art. The latter is required to be a self-contained, organized unit, bounded by a frame; the former, on the other hand, is regarded as a merely momentary or local manifestation of a ubiquitous and beginningless form. Modern art has an aesthetic emphasis, but ritual art a pedagogical-initiatory. Balance, climax, and effect, within the frame, are the characteristics of the good modern work, whereas such traits may or may not be present in the traditional masterpiece. We ask for the excitement and retention of our interest; one of the most characteristic features of traditional rites, however, is that they are rather boring and require a good deal of sitting power—sheer endurance. Many of the rituals of the Navaho are nine days long; and there is a rite in the Melanesian isle of Malekula that goes on, without interruption, for thirty-four years. We require that a work of art should yield a single effect: all should be before you; this is what we know as the principle of unity. In the great traditional rites, however, a multitude of events may take place simultaneously, no one of which is in any sense a unit; and the most important event of all, furthermore, may be developing, meanwhile, in secret—down in the Kivas of the Pueblo, or behind the iconostases of the Russian church. Obviously, if something in a context of this kind happens to appeal to our aesthetic sensibilities, this effect is accidental, and our framing of the accident deprives it of the larger portion of its sense.

FIGURE 14. Hula dancer teaching audience (United States, 2013)

Nevertheless, one cannot but observe that there is a growing tendency in modern art to seek—and actually to find—certain vital connections with the lost arts of the ancients. The poetry of the early Romantics was a prelude to this movement; James Joyce's *Finnegans Wake* is its contemporary culmination. Paul Klee best represents it in the field of the visual arts and Jean Erdman in the contemporary American dance. The fundamental idea is to restore to man a sense of relationship between the forms of his outward sensuous experience and the roots of his inward *joie de vivre.* The artwork functions symbolically to re-unite the divided modern psyche—offering to consciousness an aesthetic object while ringing, simultaneously, undertones in the unconscious. And since there is an archaic quality in the subliminal sphere (as Freud, Jung, Stekel, Róheim, and the rest have amply shown), such works, while remaining modern in the strictest sense, suggest in many ways, and often playfully parody, the timeless archetypes of the great mythological tradition. This new art has nothing to do with social propaganda, abstract form, personal exhibition, or surrealist paranoia, but is an art in which the picture frame, the bounds of the book and stage, become the new temenos—a hermetic area into which those wonderful, life-transmuting energies dance that are released in play.

The Expression of Myth
in Dance Images (1978)[1]

I WANT TO SAY A FEW WORDS on mythology in relation to the arts before coming specifically to the papers presented in this session.

It was in the middle of the nineteenth century that a distinguished anthropologist and student of these subjects, Adolf Bastian, recognized that in the mythologies and religions of the world there are constantly recurrent motifs that appear everywhere. He called these "elementary ideas," *Elementargedanken*, and they have become the subject of a number of profound psychological investigations, notably those of such great students of the human mind as Carl G. Jung and Sigmund Freud.

During the first half of the present century, the understanding, particularly in the fields of the arts, of the psychological depths sounded through mythological motifs greatly increased.[2] In the novels and poetry, for example, of such authors as Joyce, Thomas Mann, T. S. Eliot, and Yeats, as well as in the paintings of Picasso and Paul Klee, one sees how in the course of the first four decades of this century a serious fathoming and ever-deepening understanding of the human import of Bastian's elementary ideas were achieved.

Bastian recognized, however, that in every area of the world, in every culture, and in every period of history, these elementary ideas have been presented in forms peculiar to the local culture styles. One never sees an elementary idea unclothed, as it were, right out in front of one's eyes. It always appears in the costume of some specific time, place, and mentality. And he called these local forms "ethnic ideas," *Völkergedanken.*

Now it is interesting to find that Ananda K. Coomaraswamy speaks of these same two principles, the elementary and the ethnic, in Sanskrit terms. They were recognized very early in the aesthetic theories of Gupta and post-Gupta India. The elementary ideas are called in Sanskrit *mārga,* which means "the path," from the Sanskrit root *mṛg,* a root with the meaning "to search," as though following the path or tracks of an animal. And the path of the elementary idea is of the footprints of the Self, leading to

FIGURE 15. *Dōjōji* by Ippitsusai Bunchō (ink on paper, Japan, c. 1771)

the heart and soul of the individual. In other words, the universal "elementary" aspect of a myth is a guide to the believer's own deepest depths. The local inflection, the "ethnic," folk aspect, is in Sanskrit called *deśī*, which means "provincial."

Now when presenting mythic themes in the arts, in dance, in painting, or in writing, one may direct attention either to the mārga, the path to the interior depth of the individual, or to the deśī, the various local, moral, and aesthetic contexts of values. In the Chinese dance of the woman warrior, for example, there is an emphatically social, even political accent, whereas in the Japanese Dōjōji of the Noh and Kabuki theaters, the import is Japanese Buddhist, but of "the path," inasmuch as it treats of a generally human spiritual problem, namely the transformation of a bewildered, emotionally frustrated individual into a veritable devil, so trapped in phenomenal entanglements as to be inaccessible to salvation.

I found both of these papers fascinating, for they represent two completely different approaches to mythic materials, and yet in both the elementary ideas came clearly through. Evidently the dance, like myth—to use in a slightly modified way James Joyce's words with respect to tragedy—has to do with the grave and constant in human experience, even when most emphatically specific to some local culture in style and function.

Now with respect to the paper on the art of Martha Graham, it is evident that between the time of this great artist's composition of *Letter to the World* and that of *Deaths and Entrances*, she had become aware in a new way of the potentialities of a mythic inspiration. It is therefore interesting to remark that in her handling of classical themes, and in her handling also of the Celtic material of the Brontë romance, she did not place her final stress on the deśī, the historical, the local, but made use of this as a means to break us away from our own deśī, our own local entrapment, and thus release us to a larger experience of the universally human import of her themes. Thus it is that, whereas a great artist may accept inspiration from almost anywhere—either at home or abroad—he or she will strive to render through the ethnic medium an experience of some informing elementary idea. The artist will be ever concerned, also, to discipline his own feelings in relation to those ideas, and to use them then to assist the mind in following those deep, ever deeper footprints, which lead to the ultimate sources of the rapture that is the final *meaning* of art. As we read in a classical Sanskrit text on aesthetics: "As for any simple man of little intelligence who says that from dramas, which distill joy, the gain is knowledge only, as in the case of history and the like—homage to him, for he has averted his face from what is delightful" (Daśarūpa 1.6).[3]

But now, in order to render most effectively this rapture, this delight, one must learn to bring forth from one's own delight in elementary ideas appropriate forms, appropriate rhythms; for the essence of art is rhythm, nothing else: rhythms in words, rhythms in the organization of colors and forms, rhythms in body movements, and so forth. And every rhythmical structure (this is important) has a psychological implication. The great knack, if one may use such a word, of Martha Graham was her ability to find the rhythmic organization appropriate to the specific psychological references of the mythological material she was using. In that way she produced a threefold reference: the myth, its psychological sense, and the formal organization (which includes, of course, body posture) appropriate to the rendition of a certain specific psychological experience.

Now when we turn to the Noh play—its music, that strange, strange music, the wonderful slowing down of time, and the movements, gliding as though magical, and so slow that when the dancer (masked and all) moves even a little faster, it seems as though he were flying—we are in a completely mythic realm. Our experience now has nothing to do with the outside world. The images are of dream. Myth and dream: these two realms are one. Myth is the common dream, and dream is the personal myth. So that here, in the Noh, what we have is a mythic environment in the local style of a Japanese tradition. And its usual theme is the bondage of an individual to the passions, and the miracle then (or the refusal) of a spiritual release.

The reference of the Noh play is thus inward, inward to the mārga. The Noh was first associated, both in its origins and in its development, with the temple lore and festivals of medieval Buddhist Japan, and even to the present day its religious tone is retained. The Kabuki, on the other hand, is a theater of a more popular kind, with a much greater accent on entertainment; and this, of course, is another perfectly valid way to make use of mythic themes. Even with all the fun, the sensationalism and pathos, theatrical scenery and virtuosic theatrics, the mythic themes are recognizable, and they hold through.

FIGURE 16. Kiyohime transforms into a serpent (ink on paper, Japan, c. 1400)

Now I must confess, I have never seen Dōjōji as a Noh play, though I have enjoyed it many times on the Kabuki stage. Its images of the temple bell and malignant, terrible serpent are well known in the mythologies both of Europe and Asia. For example, in the Roman Catholic Mass, or in any religious ceremony, the sound of the bell (or gong) suggests the pouring of divine grace into the world. And the serpent is universally symbolic of consciousness bound to the field of terrestrial life. The serpent sheds its skin to be born again, as life throws off death to be renewed and as the moon sheds its shadow to be reborn. These two, the serpent and the moon, are equivalent symbols. Also, the serpent gliding along on its belly! What is it but a traveling esophagus? It is here to eat, as a kind of elementary life. And just so, the passions bind us to an elementary life, withholding us from release from their earthly bondage. Accordingly, the interaction of the serpent and the bell, as represented in this play, is something quite traditional in its symbolism and theme.

We turn next to the Chinese material. Here what we have is not a religious but an essentially political application of symbolic forms. Myth is susceptible to such an application, offering heroic models for this or that society to hold up as inspirations. And in our present example, the heroic aspect of the woman is what has been celebrated in a way appropriate to the requirements of a modern Communist state. Also, in the wonderful play of the Mongolian desert and steppe traditions reviewed for us by Gloria Strauss, we have again the ideal of the woman warrior. While listening to her discussion of this piece, I thought of the *Arabian Nights*. There are many tales in that great collection celebrating the woman warrior. Indeed, in oriental traditions generally, we find three dominant ideals or images of the woman, together with an occasional fourth. They are the wife and mother, mistress of the family; the courtesan, seductress, or temptress; and the amazon, the warrior and huntress; to which there is added, then, the witch. These are prominent throughout the Orient and in the Occident as well. In our own classical mythology, for example, we are familiar with Hera as the consort of Zeus, Aphrodite as the courtesan, Athena as the heroic goddess, and Hecate as the witch.

It is interesting to see how the image of the woman warrior has been handled in the literatures and mythologies of the world: Joan of Arc, for example, in Europe; the goddess Durga in Asia. She is everywhere a combination of the pair of opposites, male and female, and such a figure is psychologically fascinating. She provides a model, furthermore, for the entry of the female into fields of action proper to the male, and today, when a great range is opening of new possibilities for women in creative action, this fascinating, heroic archetype is rapidly becoming a figure of commanding interest.

The actual varieties of woman today, however, are not those (or only those) that have been traditionally represented in myth and art as typical. She is not adequately typified either as a wife, courtesan, amazon, or witch. And one of the resultant great problems, consequently, is that women now find themselves in roles for which no models are provided, developing in these their personalities, not in terms of the archetypology of any of our inherited mythic ideals, but each in terms of her own self-realization, discovering and realizing her own especial talents and possibilities. For centuries the male has had a great range of roles through which to find his way, and the female now has become eligible as well, and is ready, wanting to explore—not, however, as a pseudo-male, nor as an archetypal female, but as an individual.[4]

There is no traditional mythic support to help her in that direction. There have been, however, in the modern dance, some outstanding representatives of a bold, feminine exploration of the possibilities of life today—at least in the fields of art. And it has been my privilege, all these years, since I am married to a great dancer, to follow the careers of a number of women in their adventure of creating a new art form, a whole new realm for feminine expression and realization. For with all due respect to the males in this particular field, certainly it has been the females who have dominated the modern dance of the past century.

I am especially happy to have been given the opportunity to-day—which I have never had before—to speak in this connection of Martha Graham, whose career I have followed for some forty-odd years, recognizing there the model of a courageous, creative exploration of forms such as had never been rendered before. She took much of her own inspiration from the Orient, particularly from Japan, by way of that great creative personality of the first decades of this century, Michio Ito, and the art of Isamu Noguchi, the designer of her later sets. And this gave her the assurance of a substantial mythic background, out of which to develop her own personal adventure. For in Japan this sense of a mythic ground is very strong in *all* aspects of life—even the arrangement of flowers. Martha took that inspiration into her own life and produced from it, not an *American* dance, but Martha Graham's dance. And that is the beauty and marvel of her career.

FIGURE 17. Martha Graham in *El Penitente* (United States, 1940)

I should like to point out the great difference between what we have seen of Martha Graham's approach to classical materials and that of the ballet, as it has just been presented by Susan Au. Martha Graham seeks to bring out the profound psychological implications of her mythic themes, whereas the ballet was for centuries little more than a sort of fashionable after-dinner entertainment for people able to afford expensive evenings. I could not help thinking of Tolstoy's descriptions of the ballet in *War and Peace*, and again in *Anna Karenina*, as I was watching this rather silly representation of a deity. The classical Apollo actually is a god of a depth and sense no less profound than that of Śiva. The art-inspiring Muses are moved by the radiance of this god. He personifies the light of consciousness illuminating the universe. To present such a mythic figure in this harmless, playful way is, of course, permissible; one can do anything one likes, or that one's audience likes. But it will have nothing to do with what Apollo is actually about. The elegance of the dancing and the craft of the production may suggest something of the air of a *classical* style and form, but all this has nothing to do with Apollo, or in fact, with any god whatsoever. In contrast, we may turn, not only to the modern, personal art of Graham, but also to the Indian dance, or the manner of representing gods in any of the traditional arts of the East. Consider, for example, the image of Śiva in the Indian dance that has just been shown to us.

Let me speak for a moment of the understanding of myth in Indian art. The great devotional poem known as the Gītā Govinda of Jayadeva, the song of the god Kṛṣṇa's fascination and zeal in love for Radha, was composed at the end of the twelfth century and represents, as we have heard, the highest *bhāva*, the highest form or attitude in love.

There are five such attitudes recognized in the Indian Vaiṣṇava tradition. First, the humble attitude of the worshipper to an awe-inspiring deity. Second, that of servant to master: "Oh Lord, you are the master. Say what I am to do and I shall obey." Third, that of friend: the attitude, for example, in the Christian tradition, of the Apostles to Jesus; and in the Indian tradition of the epic Mahābhārata, the attitude of the Pandava brothers to Kṛṣṇa.

Next is the attitude of parent to child (where the deity is the child), and this accords with the birth in the heart of the love of God, which must then be fostered, as a parent should foster a child. In the Christian tradition this order of love is represented in the symbol of the Christmas Crib: our attitude toward the Christ Child. In the Vaiṣṇava tradition it is to be recognized in the attitude of the gopīs to the little butter thief, the naughty little boy Kṛṣṇa. According to the Indian view, we are in service to the Lord in this way when caring for our own children, since the divine is to be recognized in all that lives. The next stage of love is represented by the attitude of lover toward beloved. And as the highest aspect of this last stage is the ultimate attitude of unconditioned, mad, illicit love, this being the manner of Kṛṣṇa in relation to the young married matron Radha, as celebrated in Jayadeva's Gītā Govinda.

FIGURE 18. Radha and Kṛṣṇa (ink on paper, India, c. 1780)

Now it is interesting to remark that it was in exactly the same twelfth century that in Europe the romance took the form of *Tristan and Isolt.* Thomas of Britain's *Tristan* is of almost exactly the date of Jayadeva's Gītā Govinda. This example of synchronicity has something to do, not only with the universality of certain themes, but also with the mystery of a certain historical rhythm in their manifestation. For not only in Europe, but also all the way from Europe, across Asia, to Japan, this theme of love as a guide to the mystical transcendence, not only of ego, but also of all earthly bounds and bonds—the total shattering of ego and its world in an all-consuming rapture (*bhāva*)—became celebrated in poetry and art to such a degree that in India even an incarnation of God could be represented as losing himself in devotion to an earthly being.

These, then, are the five ways of interpreting in mythic terms the human sentiment that we know as love, which are illustrated and played upon in the Indian dance traditions. They are not altogether alien or unknown to our own occidental literary and mystical poets, but I cannot recall having ever seen even a hint of any of these sentiments in a modern dance.[5] Our experience of love, as of war, these days, does not include a sense of the mythic dimension. In fact, when comparing the Indian Krsna material with the European story of *Tristan,* we cannot but sense a certain depth of the former that is already lacking in our Western forms. But on the other hand, there is in our own tradition a tender human-to-human relationship between lover and beloved, which in a different way is as moving and profound as the oriental transubstantiation of the lover and beloved into deities. Our problem (and I have only occasionally seen it solved on the stage) is to bring the depth dimension of myth into view without losing our properly Western, earthly plane of vision.

FIGURE 19. *Tristan and Isolt* by George Alfred Williams (print, United States, 1909)

But the great Indian theme on which I should like, now, to terminate my talk is of the god Śiva, of whom we have just witnessed a moving and most elegant presentation. This deity is probably the oldest worshipped god in the world today, for there is evidence of a Śiva worship, or of something closely comparable, in the period of the Indus Valley Civilization of the second millennium B.C. The form of the deity best known to us is that of the beautiful, late medieval, South Indian bronzes of Naṭarāja, "Lord of the Dance," which tell the whole story of his power and operation in the world of his creation. With the beat of a drum held in his upper right hand he throws the veil of a pulse of time across the mystery of eternity, enclosing us in this time-sphere in which we live our lives. But then in his outstretched, opposite left hand is a flame that burns that veil away, the flame of Illumination, which opens to us again the vision of eternity. Meanwhile, the second right hand is in a posture that says, "Be not afraid! All that flickers on the surface of time is but a passing, phantasmagoric display." And the second left hand is pointing to the lifted left foot, signifying release, while the right foot, firmly in place on the back of a prostrate dwarf whose name means "Forgetfulness," is driving souls into life in this world, in ignorance of eternal life. Ignorance and release to illumination! The function of this art, that is to say, in throwing its own veil of rhythm and movement over the forms of this physical world, is to reveal through them an internal, eternal distance. However, in order to render the revelation of this distance, the artist himself must be standing somehow where Śiva stands: in the middle, between right and left, between the beat of time and the flame. This position is represented in the still point of the impassible head. All is moving around this head. It is symbolic of the activating source, pouring energy into the field of time, where it breaks into pairs of opposites: male and female, light and dark, right and left, and so on. In the right ear of the god is a man's earring, in the left, a woman's. And the rhythm of his form, the rhythm of this Indian artwork, which fascinates and holds us, gives us back something of the rhythm of our own aesthetic centering. Contemplated in aesthetic arrest, it may even carry us back to that silent point where all things are one and we

ourselves one with the image that we behold. So I listen to these
words and view this art from India, and it comes over me every
time: the depth, the wonder, the wisdom of that culture-world,
and how, for centuries, it has informed an art that in its perfection speaks beyond perfection to some deep distance within us.
However, it is a great problem in India today and in the Orient
today for young people in this world of rapidly changing forms
to carry anything of that unchanging message into contemporary times. To do so, the individual must sacrifice himself in a
way that is not that of our living today. And so it is that when-
ever I see these artists from India perform, I greet them with
profound respect for their dedication to an art that carries words
to us from great distances, my hope being that in our Western

FIGURE 20. Śiva Naṭarāja (bronze, India)

world we may learn from them, to translate their wisdom into living forms of our own, of our own place and time. For no one can properly take over and imitate another's rhythm. There is a rhythm in life that is theirs; there is a rhythm that is ours. They are not the same. And these are the deśī, the provincial aspects of our lives. There is a great wisdom, on the other hand, that is not provincial, but of mankind: of the elementary idea, the mārga, as India has found it, and of that we may learn, and perhaps must learn, from India.[6]

FIGURE 21. Nijinsky in *L'Après-midi d'un faune* (France, 1912)

PART II

MYTHOLOGY AND FORM
IN THE PERFORMING
AND VISUAL ARTS

CHAPTER I

———————●———————

I n   t h e   d a n c e, as in the fields of modern literature and the arts generally, the first five decades of this century exhibited on every hand the effects of a radical shift of mind in the Western World from surfaces to interiors. The solid Newtonian atom exploded. Analogously, in literature the novel dissolved through *Ulysses* to *Finnegans Wake*. In music the classical scale, and in the visual arts the shapes of things, broke up. Two world wars and a catastrophic economic depression illustrated on the historical stage an equivalent failure of trusted surfaces to hold, while in the critical field of psychology, Freud and Jung disclosed, beneath and behind the rational mind, another mind—of the living organism—with an order of aims and logic of its own.

Now it has been to the exploration and exposition of the life and order of this other, deeper, darker, so-called unconscious mind that modern literature and the creative arts have been devoted; insofar, that is to say, as they have not been consecrated, in reaction, to retaining and reworking belief systems and interests no longer realistically tenable. Inspiration and guidance for many of those turning from the exploded, breaking surfaces have lately come—and still are coming with increasing effect—from what used to be regarded as exotic sources: the philosophies, literatures, and arts of India, China, Tibet, Oceania, Africa, and pre-Columbian America. For in these, connection with the inward sources of intuitively creative life and of dream was never lost.

Accordingly, when a modern dancer, painter, sculptor, or musician deliberately sets forth upon his own uncharted, very modern Night Sea Journey, the evidences of possible ways of approach that we now have in abundance from those cultures less unsettled than our own may be taken to serve as signs. Their philosophies and arts are no longer alien curiosities, but they have been recognized as providing indications from other quarters of the globe of treasures to be searched for and found in an interior landscape that is common to mankind and which, when entered, is recognized as our own.

The distinguishing trait of the arts and philosophies (whether sacred or profane) of oriental and primitive cultures is their grounding in a mythic view of the world and of life. But the ultimate source of mythology is the human imagination, and this, in turn, as both Freud and Jung have shown, is inspired ultimately from the human unconscious. This unconscious, however, as Jung (not Freud) has shown, is of two orders: one, the "personal unconscious," which is biographically, hence historically and ethnologically, conditioned (this being the aspect to which the Freudian view is limited), and the other, the "collective" or "general unconscious," which is grounded, not in history and biography, but in anatomy and biology, in the common human central nervous system, sympathetic nervous system, and the energies of the ductless glands, not by any means the sex organs alone.[1]

Mythic symbols have been described as energy-evoking signs. Their appeal goes beyond the personal (historical-biographical) unconscious to that common (anatomical-biological) formative ground of the psyche by which all history and biography is conditioned. Formerly, the interest taken by the Western mind in the arts of oriental and primitive peoples was in their exotic, that is, historically conditioned, aspects. Since the early years of the present century, however (due largely to the intuitions of a number of visual artists, such as Manet, Gauguin, Modigliani, and Picasso), the relevance has been recognized of their formal, as distinct from exotic, aspects to the Night Sea Journey, the inward visionary quest, of the modern Western mind.

With this recognition there occurred a radical break between the arts of anecdote and of form: artworks addressed to the intellect and those touching and evoking energies from the supporting ground of the unconscious. "Art," as Cézanne has said somewhere, "is a harmony parallel to nature." The sculptor Antoine Bourdelle made the same statement in another way: "Art brings out the great lines of nature." And in the words of Aristotle: "Art is an imitation of nature"—not of nature's surfaces but of nature in its manner of operation.[2]

FIGURE 22. *Herakles the Archer* by Antoine Bourdelle (bronze, France, 1909)

Proper art (in this sense) is inward in its address: the intellect is arrested in its anecdotal discourse and held to a revelation of its own unconscious ground—to what James Joyce called an "epiphany," a revelation of the radiance of that immanent wonder which in Christological terms is known as "the Christ in us." Like the symbols of myth, the forms of such an art are thus energy-evoking signs, and between their appeal and that of myth there is a meaningful correspondence. This affinity has been recognized, not only in the visual arts, but also in literature, notably, *Ulysses* (1922) and *The Magic Mountain* (1924), *Finnegans Wake* (1939) and *Joseph and His Brothers* (1933–43). In the arts and literature of this direction, the appeal is not simply to the eye and intellect, but through the eye and intellect to those most inward centers of our nature's creative energies out of which all the great traditional arts of mankind have ever sprung, like dreams.

In the way of a working formula, the sense of this modern movement might be summarized in some such statement as the following: *In a work of proper art every aesthetic element has a psychological value equivalent to that of some mythological image or idea.* And the greatest artists, it would seem, have always known this intuitively. Critics generally have not. Nor have those artists who have allowed themselves and their art to be shaped by the journalistic mentality, which necessarily dwells in the contemplation, not of form, but of anecdote: historical, biographical, oedipal, ethical, political, or what not. Indeed, what else is there to write, paint, sing, or dance about if one's eyes and ears have not yet opened to the fascination of form, or one's mind to myth?

In the recent history of literature and the arts, the awakening of the mind to myth occurred earlier than that of the senses to form. Indeed, already at the height of the Renaissance (specifically, in 1471, with the publication of Marsilio Ficino's Latin translation of the body of Greek Gnostic writings now known

FIGURE 23. *Venus and Mars* by Botticelli (paint on canvas, Italy, 1483)

as the *Corpus Hermeticum*), the realization dawned on the greatest masters of that supreme period of Western art—Botticelli, Titian, Michelangelo, and the rest—of a timeless natural wisdom metaphorically rendered through the imagery of myth and legend. Therewith, the already lambent beauty of their works in paint and stone became imbued with the sense (in Joyce's meaning of the term) of epiphany: an intended revelation of the radiant purity of the Divine Mind—which, according to the Gnostic view, inhabits and informs all things. Of that Mind, there was nothing in the world that was not radiant, and the mind of the artist in its contemplation was an effective mirror of its informing Light.

The plane of consciousness of the mind and arts of the Renaissance, however, was consistently humanistic (Man the Measure), inspired by the recently resurrected classical arts of Greece and Rome, with Ovid and Virgil as the chief sources of relevant myths. Inevitably in such a context, literary anecdote and allegory became the illustrated subject matter throughout. The artists fixed in timeless frames of space the topic moments of the legends, and this remained the European way of relating myth to art for the next three hundred years.

But then something serious occurred.

FIGURE 24. Immanuel Kant (print, Germany, nineteenth century)

Immanuel Kant, in his *Critique of Pure Reason* (1781), demonstrated by sheer logic that the mind can know nothing of any
unconditioned, absolute *thing-in-itself*, but only phenomenal
*things conditioned by the apprehending senses and concepts condi-
tioned by the categories of thought.* Thus, there is no such thing as
objective knowledge: all knowledge is relative to and a product
of the knowing subject.

Four years later, in 1785, there appeared the first translation
into a European tongue of an Indian philosophical work—the
Bhagavad Gītā (into English by Charles Wilkins); and four years
after that, in 1789, Sir William Jones's translation of Kālidāsa's
delicious play *Śakuntalā*. Goethe, Schiller, and the whole German Romantic movement were inspired by these revelations of
an oriental mythic mode of profound philosophical and psychological insights. And then in 1801–2, a young French scholar,

Anquetil-Duperron, published a Latin translation, which he called the *Oupnek'hat*—from a Persian translation of a number of the Indian Upaniṣads. And it was from a comparison of this work with the *Critique of Pure Reason* of Kant that Schopenhauer realized that the Kantian conditioning forms of the senses and categories of thought were precisely equivalent to the Indian idea of the world-creating power known as māyā. Wagner then read Schopenhauer and, overwhelmed by its implications for his own prodigious operas based on Germanic and Arthurian myth and legend, kept the book by his side, as he tells in his autobiography, night and day.

In other words, in the brief course of the mere three score years and ten that elapsed from the publication of Kant's *Critique*, in 1781, to the lifting of the curtain on Wagner's *Der Ring des Nibelungen*, in 1852, an immense deepening and broadening of the European understanding of mythology and mythologies had occurred, involving philosophical, psychological, aesthetic, and poetic realizations of unprecedented inward implications. J.J. Bachofen's *Mother Right* followed (1861), Nietzsche's *Birth of Tragedy* (1872), and his *Thus Spake Zarathustra* (1883–84); after which, finally, as Thomas Mann points out in his essay on "Freud and the Future" (1936), the psychiatrists Freud and Jung, and the schools of analysts following, translated the import of the intuitive achievements of these German Romantics into the medical terms of a therapeutic technique.

So much, then, for the modern understanding of myth.

CHAPTER 2

———————●———————

FOR THE MODERN APPRECIATION of the mystery of form, the center of realization was Paris and the leading medium, painting—commencing with the opening in 1863 of the Salon des Refusés, for the exhibition of those artists who had radically broken with the Neoclassical and Romantic criterions of the Académie des Beaux-Arts. Such names as Monet, Manet, Pissarro, Renoir, and Degas typify this stage of the movement. The next was the achievement, uniquely, of Cézanne, in the structured canvases of whose mature period—from 1888 or so to 1905—the founding model was given for the realization of painterly form in the twentieth century.

Turning his back both on the narrative scenes of the Neoclassicists and Romantics, and on the representations of nature in its appearances by his friends the Impressionists, Cézanne labored to render on canvas, not a reproduction of the appearance of a scene, but a stable structure in paint reflecting his own empathy with its informing harmony. Behind the māyā-veil of the appearances of things, he recognized another order: "Everything in nature is modeled after the sphere, the cone, and the cylinder. One must learn to paint from these simple figures."

FIGURE 25. *Still Life with Apples* by Cézanne (paint on canvas, France, 1893–94)

Braque, Picasso, and the rest picked up from there. From the humanistic plane of interest—with its voluptuous imagery and edifying themes—a breakthrough had been achieved to a plane of disinterested, transpersonal contemplation, to which Gauguin then brought from Oceania suggestions of a way in which mythic elements might be introduced into a canvas without violating the integrity of its formal idiom. In *The Moon and the Earth* (1893), *Day of the God* (1894), and *Where Do We Come From? What Are We? Where Are We Going?* (1897), the forms of Polynesian temple images appeared, not as illustrations of known narratives, but as affect images of unknown import, opening through the eye intimations of a background of mystery that is normally veiled from the eye, though immanent in oneself and throughout nature, here made known through the window of art.

FIGURE 26. *Les Demoiselles d'Avignon* by Picasso (paint on canvas, France, 1907)

The next season of years saw mythology from every quarter of the globe breaking into canvases, until, in 1907, another capital moment in the history of modern painting was marked by the young Picasso's incorporation of features from an African mask in the composition of a work—*Les Demoiselles d'Avignon*—that had been inspired initially by one of Cézanne's late *Bathers* scenes. The astonishing *Nude with Raised Arms* followed in the autumn of the same year, where the usual requirement for a visual reference to some studio setting or natural scene is ignored and the painted canvas itself has become the self-sufficient envisioned field of an aesthetically generated apparition. The title, the following year, of a related creation, *The Dryad* (1908), hints at the artist's recognition of possible mythic counterparts of these otherwise unprecedented appearances. However, there is nothing of intentional mythologizing discoverable in either his productions or his titles of the following ten years, 1909–1919, where the interest is, rather, in boldly analytical and synthetic structural arrangements, continuing to every possible extreme the initial formal impulse of Cézanne.

From 1920, on the other hand, following the end of World War I (Act I of Europe's paranoiac twentieth-century spectacular of self-immolation), Picasso's choice of subjects over which to pass the magic of his brush became increasingly mythic and metaphysical themes: enigmatic female appearances, racing, dancing, or seated on beaches against backgrounds of sand and a timeless sea; or violent episodes from the Spanish bullring, showing, now the bull, now the picador horse, now a picador or matador (female with exposed breasts), as the immolated victim. A painting of the Crucifixion represents the picador's lance as the lance that pierced Christ's side. And from the year 1933, in a powerful series of fantasized scenes, the ominous figure of the Cretan Minotaur appears, now as the bull of the bullring, now a lusty companion of philosophers in lechery, or now, mysteriously blind, guided by a little girl in the night. The ambiguous monster first appeared on the cover of the first issue of a luxurious art magazine *Minotaure* (June 1, 1933), seated, holding up a threatening knife with its blade ironically shaped like a living leaf. Two years later, in a series of engravings entitled *Minotauromachy*, an assemblage of these recurrent figures comes together in a scene symbolic—ominously—of the whole threat of the nightmare of our century; and again two years later, in *Guernica* (1937), the prophecy is fulfilled.

Picasso's art in those years was formally appropriate to the reception and manipulation of apocalyptic mythic themes. The man himself was psychologically so attuned to the tremendous tensions and explosions of his age that in his art there is a perfect

FIGURE 27. *Guernica* by Picasso (paint on canvas, France, 1937)

accord of energy, image, and apocalypse. During roughly the same span of years, the whimsical Swiss painter Paul Klee was also dealing with mythic themes, but in a more open, less committed way. Myths were not drawn into his art; his art was drawn into the myths, altering in style, medium, and formal organization according to the affect value of the inspiring mythic suggestion of the moment. We are told that as a child of four, he would seek refuge near his mother when the devils he was scrawling on scraps of paper seemed to him to come to life. This same openness to seizure by the figments of his own imagination animates each of his thousands of later productions with an immediacy of presence, which—in spite of their apparent innocence and disarming wit—drives them home as experiences of that universe within which we have always known.

Both of Klee's parents were musicians. At seven he began his study of the violin. His pictures have a distinctly musical quality that is quite apart from the architecturally (spatially) structured tradition out of Cézanne. In the *Pedagogical Sketchbook* that he prepared for instruction of his students at the State Bauhaus in Weimar, he interpreted and illustrated in detail the rhythmic and affect values of lines, colors, geometrical organizations, juxtapositions, balances, and relationships. Like the movements seen

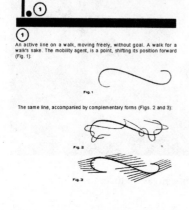

FIGURE 28. Figure from *Pedagogical Sketchbook* by Paul Klee (print, Germany, 1925)

today (in the great physics laboratories) of subatomic particles, flashing, passing and vanishing, out of and into an unknown, the unsubstantial figures of his inspiration are of energies in passage, musically, in a field at float on a void. There are no crises of development in the history of his studio. His models were not in the space of the world but of the mind, sprung from the heart. "The heart," he is reported to have taught, "must do its work undisturbed by reflective consciousness." And again: "Form often develops of its own free will and strives to dominate with ever-increasing authority. Only with great effort can the artist control it....I always preferred doing nothing until the purity of form was assured and work forced itself upon me."

"All true creation is a thing born of nothing."[1]

Every one of Klee's productions, consequently, is an exemplar of that principle already announced—of every aesthetic element in a work of proper art having a psychological value equivalent to that of some mythological image or idea. The sustaining mythological idea of Klee's creativity was of phenomenality:

the metamorphic play of the unsubstantial names and forms of mankind's world of outward and inward experience over an unknown. When about twenty-two (in 1901), together with Hermann Haller, a sculptor, Klee had made the conventional artist's pilgrimage to Italy, but what there overcame him, more than all the monuments, *palazzi*, and Renaissance churches, was a visit paid to the Aquarium at Naples. There (as one of his biographers has told) "in a darkened room the unearthly world of the ocean appeared behind glass windows, close enough to make one feel the breath and the life of this monstrous fauna and weirdly demonic flora. How fascinating to watch a flower's transformation into an animal and to discover a rock to be a turtle or an old mossy fish. Klee was struck to meet in tangible form phantoms and apparitions he had envisioned as a child and which had impelled his imagination toward creative endeavor.

"Here he found greater attraction than in the glorious remains of history. The more he felt them to be dead and gone, the more he grew aware of the emptiness and imitativeness of his own epoch, which made him feel depressed and ill at ease. When he came back to Munich, his friends found him changed and given to meditation."[2]

The world under waves of the unconscious and the creative sea had come together: worlds at once of the creative imagination and the universal womb of nature. And it should be there, in Paul Klee's view, not in the shapes of things already become, whether of history or of nature, that the artist should seek his source. "It is not my task to reproduce appearances," he wrote in a diary notation of that year, "for that there is the photographic plate—I want to penetrate into the inmost meaning of the model. I want to reach the heart."[3]

Compare the words of the aged Goethe to his secretary, the young Eckermann, in their conversation of Friday, February 13, 1829: "The Godhead is effective in the living and not in the dead, in the becoming and the changing, not in the become and the set-fast; and therefore, similarly, the reason (*Vernunft*) is concerned only to strive toward the divine through the becoming and the living, and the understanding (*Verstand*) only to make use of the become and the set-fast."[4]

FIGURE 29. *Minotaur* by Picasso (pencil drawing with pasted papers and cloth tacked on wood, France, 1935)

Finally, of course, that is the meaning, also, of the knife, shaped like a living leaf, held lifted in the hand of Picasso's Minotaur: also, of the little plant seen growing, foreground-center, in his *Guernica*, by the hand holding the broken sword of the hollow image, broken by the bomb; and the bull, meanwhile, with his seeing eye, stands calm and secure. Clearly, behind and beyond the obvious surface reading, political, ethical, or historical, of an artwork of this popular kind, there must be another, of a different order, touching an objective insight into the nature of reality in its manner of operation or becoming. And therein is the way of the passage through art to myth, or from myth to art.

CHAPTER 3

———•———

THE YEARS OF THE FIRST WORLD WAR were richly productive of realizations of this order. The evident insanity of what had been thought to be a continent of civilized nations pouring its young manhood onto such slaughter fields as the world had never before known filled minds unconvinced by the various local arguments with a loathing for the whole system of practical reason that had brought this debacle about. In 1916, a summons to contrary acts of *unreason*—nicknamed Dada—was issued by a group of young artists and war resisters meeting at Hugo Ball's Cabaret Voltaire in Zurich. Dada caught on, spreading to Paris and Berlin, Cologne, Hanover, and presently, New York: at first, mainly in the way of impudent gestures of insult to the champions of rationality. But then, as it became increasingly evident that its intentionally infantile pranks, which were having no effect whatsoever upon the established social order, were nevertheless infallibly catalytic of irrational individuals, Dada opened into Surrealism: a combined artistic and literary movement, chiefly of the 1920s, where, in contrast to the negativism of Dada, a positive approach was taken to the provocation of irrational responses. For these, it was now apparent, were out of the same psychological unconscious that Freud and Jung were exploring. (Jung, by the way, was living in Zurich, as was also, at that time, James Joyce.) In 1920, Tristan Tzara, one of the

Künstlerkneipe Voltaire

Allabendlich (mit Ausnahme von Freitag)

Musik-Vorträge und Rezitationen

Eröffnung Samstag den 5. Februar

im Saale der „Meierei" Spiegelgasse 1

FIGURE 30. Poster for Cabaret Voltaire by Marcel Słodki (print, Switzerland, 1916)

originators of Dada, came to Paris. (Picasso's art, we have seen, opened that year to mythology: Klee was at work, at the time, in Munich.) And four years later, the poet and critic André Breton issued in Paris a Marxian parody, called *The Surrealist Manifesto*, in which the aim of the movement was declared to be the realization of such a confluence of unconscious and conscious forms that the realities of dream and rational practicality should finally be united in "an absolute reality, a surreality."

How seriously all this was intended, it is impossible to estimate. There is a quality of spoof about the whole affair. But in any case, it was Freud's theory of the unconscious (not Jung's) that was in those days in fashion, so that the movement developed in an ambience, rather of the "personal, biographical-historical unconscious," than of the "collective, biologically grounded." Its productions, consequently, have the quality rather of dream than of myth, and their psychological interest rests chiefly in erotically symptomatic anecdote. The painting styles are, accordingly, illustrative and illusionist—at their best suggesting products of a Neoclassic or Romantic brush applied to images rather of dream-life than of day. And as for aesthetic form, there is little to choose between the paintings of Maxfield Parrish and the "hand-painted dream photographs" of the Surrealist Salvador Dalí.

Dalí's paintings were produced, as the artist himself had declared, in states of erotic delirium induced by his special "paranoiac critical method." In such states, as he tells, dream invades reality and reality turns into dream, in consequence of a startling "crisis of the object": some bizarre association or distortion. For example, to a canvas entitled *Soft Self-Portrait with Fried Bacon* he has supplied the following commentary: "Anti-psychological self-portrait; instead of painting the soul—the *inside*—I wanted to paint solely the outside: the envelope, 'the glove of myself.' This glove of myself is edible, and even a little gamey; this is why ants are shown, together with a strip of bacon."[1] Such associations are, of course, emphatically personal.

FIGURE 31. *The Sacrament of the Last Supper* by Salvador Dalí (paint on canvas, Spain, 1955)

But mythological and religious subjects have also been handled in the same illusionist style and with suggestive associations; for example, as in this artist's re-creation of Leonardo da
Vinci's *The Last Supper*.

In sum, then, for the modern visual arts, we may record on
the two sides of our comparative ledger, first, on the anecdotal,
illustrational side, four ways of interpreting mythic elements:

1. the Iconographic of the Gothic Middle Ages, as continued in the art, for example, of Rouault;
2. the Neoclassical, continuous from the period of the
   Renaissance;
3. the Romantic, from the late eighteenth and early nineteenth centuries; and
4. following the rupture of the First World War, the Surrealist, where either classical or Christian images might
   appear in some context of either overt or covert erotic
   allusion;

and on the more formally aesthetic side, principally two
ways of handling mythic motifs or themes:

1. that represented by Picasso, where an appropriate mythol-
   ogem is brought into and assimilated to an aesthetic
   organization; and
2. that represented by Klee, where it is an experienced sense
   of the mythic theme that constellates the aesthetic organization.

There may, of course, be other ways in which this problem has been solved, of which I am unaware—in the modern
arts, for example, of Japan, India, or China—but in the main, I
think, these six ways of bringing mythic matter into the modern
painting about cover the field.

CHAPTER 4

———————•———————

THE THEATRICAL ARTS, both of classical Greece and of medieval Europe, were developed out of rituals grounded in mythology. In Greece, according to Aristotle, the beginnings were in the dithyramb: a ritual of dance and song in celebration of the dying and resurrected god Dionysos. While our earliest evidence of an enacted scene from medieval Europe is in a Latin manuscript of the ninth century known as the "*Quem quaeritis* (Whom seek ye) *Trope*": a brief text sung by two divisions of the choir during mass on Easter Sunday, when members of the local clergy enacted the Gospel scene (from Mark 16:1–8) of the three Marys at the tomb of the Risen Christ:

> Angels at the tomb: Whom seek ye in the sepulcher, O followers of Christ?
> The Marys: Jesus of Nazareth, who was crucified, O celestial ones.
> Angels: He is not here; he is risen, just as he foretold. Go, announce that he is risen from the sepulcher.

Likewise, in Japan from the eleventh century or so, little plays were enacted within the compounds of Buddhist temples, and by the fourteenth and fifteenth centuries, out of these beginnings had developed the elegant, highly stylized theater of the Noh, where mask and mime, an extremely stately dance, flute tones, drum taps, and choral song unite to render an experience of suggested beauty beyond that beheld by the eye.

FIGURE 32. Noh theater by Torii Kiyomitsu (polychrome woodblock print on paper, Japan, c. 1763)

Whereas in both Greece and Japan the theater retained its formality, however, and along with this connection with mythology and legend, in Europe a progressive trend toward secular themes led finally (by the middle of the nineteenth century) to a transfer of interest from mythology and legend to history and biography and, along with this, a dismissal of stylization and relaxation into naturalism.

The experience and understanding of myth as the language of man's spiritual life had, in fact, been lost. Truly serious theater should deal with existential agonies; adult entertainment, with erotic spectacles and comedies; while the inward, spiritual life was something to be attended to in churches, having to do (it was supposed), not with mythology, but with a true history of incredible (hence spiritual) events, as reported (by God himself) in the Bible.

FIGURE 33. *The Lower Depths* by Maxim Gorky (Russia, 1902)

When, toward the opening of the twentieth century, the new understanding of the import of mythology was inspiring poets and artists alike, there was little in the way of models for the stage to inspire and support playwrights. The towering achievement of Goethe's *Faust* (from 1829) was literally out of sight: no one knew how to stage part 2, or even to translate the play effectively out of German into any other tongue. Though Wagner's operas had opened a magnificent view toward the possibilities of Celtic and Germanic myth, the leading playwrights of the period had their minds turned, rather, to Emile Zola's call (in 1867) for a theater dedicated, like the novels of his time, to a faithful recording of human behavior and the scientific analysis of life. As examples of the result, we may think of the plays of Chekhov and Gorky, Ibsen, Strindberg, Bjørnson, Hauptmann, Wedekind, Becque, and George Bernard Shaw.

There began presently to appear, however, breaks in this prosaic scene with signs of a realization, not only that there may be more to the mystery of life than meets the scientific eye, but also that art is not at its best as a branch of science. In 1888, Ibsen in *The Lady from the Sea* moved from his expressly social, problematical, and moralist earlier form of drama—*Pillars of Society, A Doll's House, Ghosts,* etc.—to a more psychological and visionary, symbolic style. There followed *Hedda Gabler* (1890), *The Master Builder* (1892), *Little Eyolf* (1894), *John Gabriel Borkman* (1896), and *When We Dead Awaken* (1899). In 1898, Strindberg, following a season of mental agony that culminated in a religious crisis, broke from his earlier, starkly naturalistic, socio-critical dramatic mode—represented in *The Father, Miss Julie,* and *Creditors*—with the publication of parts 1 and 2 of his semi-autobiographical play *To Damascus.* Then came *The Dance of Death* (1900), *A Dream Play* (1902), and (after a number of others) *The Ghost Sonata* (1907), in which motifs appear from Wagner united with themes from Hindu and Buddhist thought.[1]

FIGURE 34. Max Reinhardt's production of *A Midsummer Night's Dream* (United States, 1935)

In Germany at this time, the brilliant productions of Max Reinhardt were illustrating the possibilities of sheer theater when the weight of naturalism is unloaded and the imagination of a courageously creative director is let soar. His production in 1905, when he was twenty-eight, of Shakespeare's *A Midsummer Night's Dream* established his spectacular career. Swift, light, and joyous in its action and delivery of lines, it broke entirely with tradition and was attacked by the usual critics for "theatricality." Six years later, with *The Miracle*, he transformed London's huge Olympia exhibition building into a cathedral, so that the audience became part of the congregation, and with a cast of over two thousand actors, musicians, dancers, and other personnel, without a word of dramatic dialogue, he rendered a medieval miracle of the Virgin in a modern reunification, not only of drama with the mythic mode, but also of dance, music, visual setting, and dramatic action.[2]

The idea of a theater represented in such a production was something very different from the pseudo-scientific revelation in a simulated living room of some painful or amusing family secret. The incorporation of music, mime, and dance lifted the entertainment from the living room to a space of the imagination, where mere fact became transparent of a rapture. Gordon Craig, in England, was writing at that time of an ideal for a *future* theater that was very much like the one that Reinhardt was already producing, and in some of his most waspish articles, written under various pseudonyms in his own quarterly journal, *The Mask*, he directly accused the German of having peeked over his shoulder and stolen his ideas.[3]

Actually, Craig's ideas for the future were considerably more modest than Max Reinhardt's present accomplishments, but in the main they were of the same poetic order. There is a word from William Blake that Craig quoted in one of his numerous pieces published in 1912, which gives the clue to what is required for the creation of such an art, namely, as follows: "All forms are perfect in the poet's mind, but these are not abstracted or compounded from nature; they are from the imagination."[4]

Craig's idea and Reinhardt's accomplishment were of what has since been called "Total Theater" (Craig's term): a stage combining the several arts of acting, makeup, scenic design, lighting, and music, with a single director responsible for harmonizing the whole to a unified aesthetic effect. But this, exactly, is what Japan had already created in the Noh, as well as in the more popular Kabuki. And so, was it then only by chance or possibly, rather, by a miracle of the mystery that C. G. Jung has called Synchronicity—that an extraordinarily gifted and attractive young Japanese student of the performing arts arrived in Europe, at just this time, to study opera?

CHAPTER 5

———————◆———————

MICHIO ITO (1893–1961) came first to Paris, where he discovered that opera singers in Europe performed standing still. This was hardly what he had had in mind when he left Japan to study singing in the West. He saw Isadora Duncan dance, however; also, a performance by Nijinsky; and in his search for his own direction, met and consulted with both Rodin and Debussy. Where he came to rest, at last, however, was in Germany, studying and practicing eurythmics in the recently founded school of Émile Jaques-Dalcroze at Hellerau, near Dresden.

Those critical years of Ito's life were 1911 to 1914; his age, eighteen to twenty-one. Then came the war, and he was advised to go to London, where, by chance (by chance?), when on the point of starvation (three days on one bowl of soup), he was taken by a British friend to a party at the fashionable home of Lady Ottoline Morrell, and there, before a company that included George Bernard Shaw, William Butler Yeats, T. Sturge Moore, and Lord Asquith (Prime Minister of England), outfitted in a scraped-together costume of Turkish trousers and a short Spanish jacket and accompanied on the piano by the conductor of the Queen's Hall Orchestra—he performed to a Chopin Prelude a brief dance that he had composed for his examination at the Dalcroze School.[1]

FIGURE 35. Michio Ito (France, 1919)

And with that there was inaugurated a career:

A brilliant career of four and a half decades (1914–61), significantly influential in the performing arts of three continents—Europe, North America, and Asia—not only through its transcendence of regionalism, East and West, by way of its recognition of the universal principles both of art and of human movement, but also as a consequence of Ito's own extraordinary ability to suggest, through the imagery of his dance structures, backgrounds or implications of a mythic kind! "He was able," wrote Yeats, "as he rose from the floor...or as he threw out an arm, to recede from us into some more powerful life."[2]

"All art," as Yeats has stated, "is the disengagement of a soul from place and history."[3] The young Ito's period of study with Dalcroze had been exactly right for the launching of a life in art transcendent, thus, of the naturalism of regional and ethnic limitations. As pointed out by Helen Caldwell, Ito's biographer and former student, in Japan he had studied the popular Kabuki, where drama, music, and dance are combined, as they are, also, in eurythmics.[4] In neither discipline, however, was the narrative aspect the basic concern, but the formal; and the formal, furthermore, inspired by an idea. "Gesture itself is nothing," we read in Dalcroze's own words. "Its whole value depends on the idea, the emotion that inspires it."[5] And from Michio Ito's Orient we hear everywhere the same.

For, as Ananda K. Coomaraswamy has pointed out, from China "a multitude of texts could be adduced to show that it is not the outward appearance (*hsing*) which is to be exhibited as such, but rather the idea (*i*) in the mind of the artist, or the immanent divine spirit (*shen*), or breath of life (*ch'i*), that is to be revealed by a use of natural form directed to this end."[6]

Likewise, in India the first requirement of the artist is to become expert in "contemplative vision" (*yoga-dhyāna*), the whole procedure of his art then being summed up in the words *dhyātvā kuryāt*, "when the visualization has been realized (*dhyātvā*), set to work (*kuryāt*)."[7]

Dalcroze's fundamental intention, expressed in his own words, was "to create by the help of rhythm a rapid and regular current between brain and body," the understanding being that in this way the conscious and unconscious orders of the mind are brought to accord, the current of energy flowing from one to the other being experienced, then, as euphoria.

This idea is the same, essentially, as that expressed by James Joyce, where he writes of the "rhythm of beauty" as the effective element in all art that is properly art (and not simply artistry in the service of either pornography or didacticism). For it is alone this realization of harmony, *the relationship of part to part, of each part to the whole, and of the whole to each of its parts*, that arrests the mind ("aesthetic arrest") and enchants the heart in the aesthetic form.[8]

Dalcroze's way of achieving such a harmony was to coordinate precisely body movements to musical rhythms, giving in this way plastic physical expression to fugues, symphonies, and operas, note values being indicated by movements of the feet and body, time values by the arms. Out of this idea the Russian mystical philosopher Gurdjieff developed his system of precisely rhythmed movement-meditations for the centering and harmonization of his disciples, overpassing thereby their personal, variously subjective systems of sentiments and ideas to reach the common—or, as he termed it, the "objective"—ground of their creaturely being. And comparably, but very differently, Michio Ito composed, as an artist, two orders of stylized arm, body, leg, and foot movements and positions to constitute a modern dance style more flexible and natural to the body than that of the sixteenth-century classical ballet.

CHAPTER 6

———•———

ALREADY A DECADE EARLIER THAN ITO, the American Isadora Duncan, by whom he had been first inspired, had challenged the artificialities of that fashionable artifact of the Late Renaissance. Inspired by an enthusiastic study of the forms of the truly classical dance represented on Greek vases in the British Museum, she had stepped forth, barefoot, uncorseted, and as scantily clad as a woodland nymph, to electrify the concert halls of Europe. In 1905, in Russia, the art critic Diaghilev was impressed, and in 1909 he arrived in Paris with his company, the Ballets Russes, already inspired by her influence. So that at the time of Michio Ito's formulation of his modern dance style, three varieties of so-called classical dance were already on the scene: the revolutionary, of Isadora Duncan; the conservative, of Anna Pavlova; and the romantic, of Diaghilev's Ballets Russes.

Pavlova in 1909 had separated from Diaghilev with a company of her own and toured the world with a repertoire largely of such conventional compositions as *The Fairy Doll, Giselle, Don Quixote,* and *La Fille mal gardée,* to which she added the enchantment of her own ephemeral, yet immortal, solos: *Gavotte, The Dragonfly, Californian Poppy,* and what became her signature piece, *The Dying Swan,* which had been composed for her in 1905 by Mikhail Fokine, Diaghilev's first choreographer.

FIGURE 36. Isadora Duncan (United States, c. 1916–18)

To the world, she represented the last miracle of the old tsar-
ist Imperial School of Ballet, while Diaghilev and the company
from which she had separated moved into the modern period
with a triad of new works inspired by the advanced music of
Stravinsky—*The Firebird* (1910), *Petrushka* (1911), and *The Rite
of Spring* (1913)—so advanced, indeed, that when the last of
these was first performed at the Théâtre des Champs-Élysées,
its fashionable French audience broke into an uproar that so
outdid the polyphony of the orchestra that Nijinsky, the choreographer, to keep his company on beat, stood on a chair in
the wings, gesticulating and shouting to the rhythm while the
undaunted group carried on.

    Diaghilev's ideal had been to achieve an integration of dance
and mime, music, drama, and visual design as a "total work of
art" in which no one element should dominate over the others,
and in this masterwork he succeeded—only two years after Max
Reinhardt's production of *The Miracle*, of similar intent, though

from a point of origin, rather, of theater than of dance. And in both triumphs, it is interesting to note, the inspiration had been derived (as in the earlier triumphs of Wagner on the opera stage) from mythology.

Meanwhile, in the British Isles, the poet whom T. S. Eliot called "the greatest of our time...in any language" was contemplating a completely different approach to the turning of myth into Total Theater. W. B. Yeats, who in 1904, in association with Lady Gregory, had opened the Abbey Theatre in Dublin, was, in the matter of mythology, certainly the most learned poet— or indeed artist in any field—at that time living. A magnificent generation of the best scholarship had within his lifetime edited, translated, correlated, and interpreted the major documents of the epic literatures of pagan and early Christian Ireland. Sir James G. Frazer's *The Golden Bough*, completed and published in twelve volumes (1890–1915) had opened to common view the whole great range, through space and time, of the myths and rituals of mankind. Yeats had himself collected, studied, and admired the folk traditions of the Irish peasantry. He was learned in oriental lore, as well as in the occult, and, moreover, understood how to translate into poetry the messages of their recondite wisdom language. He was thus no longer looking for material and themes to shape into his art, but searching for an art through which to render what he knew to be the messages for contemporary man of these great heritages of which he had become the carrier.

It was an important moment, both for Yeats and for the history of modern letters, therefore, when Ezra Pound, the most learned and gifted *American* literary man of his generation, introduced him, in 1913, to Ernest Fenollosa's translations of a number of Japanese Noh plays. Pound had been asked by the great orientalist's widow to edit her husband's literary remains, and among the manuscripts were these plays. The two poets were fascinated. Yeats immediately began considering the idea of putting the formalities of Noh to use, somehow, in the service of his own mythologically grounded art. And so, he was already well into the subject when, a year later, Michio Ito arrived and performed his graduation piece in Lady Ottoline Morrell's drawing room.

FIGURE 37. Michio Ito as the Hawk in *At the Hawk's Well* (England, c. 1916)

When Pound learned of the occasion, he invited Ito to help him with the editing of the manuscripts. It was then he learned that there were two young Japanese in London who had been Ito's classmates in Tokyo and could demonstrate something of the drum and vocal tones that contribute to the special atmosphere of a Noh performance. Yeats, inspired, set seriously to work, and in 1916, two years into the First World War, produced in a London drawing room, with Michio Ito as dancer against a simple set of panels by Gordon Craig, the first of his mythological plays for dancers, *At the Hawk's Well*.[1]

Yeats's own first comment to Lady Gregory is interesting, one week before the first performance: "I believe I have at last found a dramatic form that suits me."[2]

The form was the very opposite of that represented in such vast affairs as Diaghilev's *The Rite of Spring* and Reinhardt's *The Miracle*. It was, rather, of a theater of intimacy, or of no theater at all, but of such a drawing room for a small company as that in which the Dalcroze examination piece had been performed. Yeats wrote in an essay describing this new idea of a theater:

> I have written a little play that can be played in a room for so little money that forty or fifty readers of poetry can pay the price. There will be no scenery, for three musicians, whose seeming sunburned faces will, I hope, suggest that they have wandered from village to village in some country of our dreams, can describe place and weather, and at moments action and accompany it all by drum and gong or flute and dulcimer. Instead of the players working themselves into a violence of passion indecorous in our sitting-room, the music, the beauty of form and voice all come to climax in pantomimic dance....
>
> I love all the arts that can still remind me of their origin among the common people, and my ears are only comfortable when the singer sings as if mere speech had taken fire, when he appears to have passed into song almost imperceptibly. I am bored and wretched, a limitation I greatly regret, when he seems no longer a human being but an invention of science.... The human voice can only become louder by becoming less articulate, by discovering some new musical sort of roar or scream. As poetry can do neither, the voice must be freed from this competition and find itself among little instruments, only heard at their best perhaps when we are close about them....
>
> My play is made possible by a Japanese dancer whom I have seen dance in a studio and in a drawing room and on a very small stage lit by an excellent stage-light. In the studio and in the drawing room alone, where the lighting was the light we are most accustomed to, did I see him as the tragic image that has stirred my imagination. There, where no studied lighting, no stage-picture made an artificial world, he was able, as he rose from the floor, where he had been sitting cross-legged, or as he threw out an arm, to recede from us into some more powerful life. Because that separation was achieved by human means alone, he receded but to inhabit as it were the deeps of the mind. One realized anew, at every separating strangeness, that the measure of all the arts' greatness can be but in their intimacy.[3]

And what his new form of art meant to his reputation as a poet may be judged from the comment, years later, of T. S. Eliot. "Yeats was well known, of course," he wrote in an article on Ezra Pound in *Poetry* (September 1946).[4] "But to me, at least, Yeats did not appear, until after 1917 [read 1916], to be anything but a minor survivor of the '90s. After that date, I saw him differently. I remember well the impression of the first performance of *The Hawk's Well*, in a London drawing room, with a celebrated Japanese dancer in the role of the hawk, to which Pound took me. And thereafter one saw Yeats rather as a more eminent contemporary than as an elder from whom one could learn."

"Ito, for his part," as Helen Caldwell learned, "was so impressed by the poetic beauty and dramatic power of *At the Hawk's Well* that he presented it twice in the United States, in New York in 1918 and in California in 1929. In 1939 he translated the play into Japanese for performance in Japan, where it ultimately came to be regarded as a genuine Noh play and was made a part of Japan's permanent Noh repertory."[5]

On the other hand, the mask and its aesthetic force became for Yeats increasingly interesting as he worked his way into the creative task of rendering mythic ideas on his intimate stage; and with the model of the Noh now in mind, he believed he had learned how to use it. "A mask will enable me to substitute for the face of some commonplace player, or for that face repainted to suit his own vulgar fancy, the fine invention of a sculptor, and to bring the audience close enough to the play to hear every inflection of the voice," he wrote in his 1916 article, written immediately after his *Hawk's Well* performance. "In poetical painting and in sculpture the face seems the nobler for lacking curiosity, alert attention, all that we sum up under the famous word of the realists, 'vitality.' It is even possible that being is only possessed completely by the dead, and that it is some knowledge of this that makes us gaze with so much emotion upon the face of the Sphinx or of Buddha."[6] In the Noh, he declared, he had discovered an ideal dramaturgical model that would synthesize the "pulse of life" with the "stillness of death"[7]—which, finally, it may now be said, is exactly the great synthesis of opposites that it is the function of both art and mythology—to render as an affect image to the eye of the mind. With this, the *formal* principle in art—known in painting, sculpture, architecture, and music as *the rhythm of beauty* and the indispensable catalyst of aesthetic arrest—came finally into place in the art (lost in naturalism) of the English theater.

CHAPTER 7

———————————•———————————

THE INTRODUCTION to the *American* theater of a serious realization of the aesthetic value of visual (not simply narrative)
form was the achievement principally of a dozen courageous
dancers. The movement can be said to have commenced with
Isadora Duncan's quest in the late 1890s for a form of dance
more natural to the body and its life than the mannered court
style of the ballet. In her own words: "When I was fifteen years
old and I realized that there was no teacher in the world who
could give me any help in my desire to be a dancer, because at
that time the only school that existed was the ballet, I turned,
as I had noticed all other artists except dancers do, to the study
of nature."[1]

"Woman is not a thing apart and separate from all other
life, organic and inorganic. She is but a link in a chain, and her
movement must be one with the great movement which runs
through the universe; and therefore the fountain-head for the
art of the dance will be the study of the movements of Nature."[2]

In 1903–4 she visited Greece and, standing before the Parthenon, "this monument," as she called it, "of the one immortal
Beauty," lifting her eyes to the rhythmical succession of Doric
columns, she felt form, as she once told an audience, "in its fin-
est and noblest sense."

FIGURE 38. Isadora Duncan at the Parthenon (Greece, c. 1921)

She declared:

For the last four months, each day I have stood before this miracle of perfection wrought of human hands. I have seen around it sloping the Hills, in many forms, but in direct contrast to them the Parthenon, expressing their fundamental idea. *Not in imitation of the outside forms of nature, but in understanding of nature's great secret rules, rise the Doric columns.*

The first days as I stood there my body was as nothing and my soul was scattered; but gradually called by the great inner voice of the Temple, came back the parts of myself to worship it: first came my soul and looked upon the Doric columns, and then came my body and looked—but in both were silence and stillness, and I did not dare to move, for I realized that of all the movements my body had made none was worthy to be made before a Doric Temple. And as I stood thus I realized that I must find a dance whose effort was to be worthy of this Temple—or never dance again.

Neither Satyr nor Nymph had entered here, neither Shadows nor Bacchantes. All that I had danced was forbidden in this Temple—neither love nor hate nor fear, nor joy nor sorrow—only a rhythmic cadence, those Doric columns—only in perfect harmony this glorious Temple, calm through all the ages.

> For many days no movement came to me. And then one day came the thought: These columns which seem so straight and still are not really straight, each one is curving gently from the base to the height, each one is in flowing movement, never resting, and the movement of each is in harmony with the others. And as I thought this my arms rose slowly toward the Temple and I leaned forward—and then I knew I had found my dance, and it was a Prayer.[3]

She never thought of her dance as Greek, however; nor as of the past; but of America, its future, and the world. "It has often caused me to smile, but somewhat bitterly, when people have called my dancing Greek," she wrote in 1927. "For I count its origin in the stories which my Irish Grandmother often told us of crossing the plains with Grandfather in '49 in a covered wagon she eighteen, he twenty-one....All this Grandmother danced in the Irish Jig; and I learnt it from her, and put it into my own aspiration of Young America." Walt Whitman's poem "I Hear America Singing" had then inspired her to a vision of her own: "I See America Dancing." "And that," she declared, "is the origin of the so-called Greek dance with which I have flooded the world.[4]

"That was the origin, the root," her analysis continued. "But afterwards, coming to Europe, I had three great Masters, the three great precursors of the Dance of our century, Beethoven, Nietzsche, and Wagner. Beethoven created the Dance in a mighty rhythm, Wagner in sculptural form, Nietzsche in spirit. Nietzsche created the dancing philosopher.

"I often wonder where is the American composer who will hear Walt's America singing, and who will compose the true music for the American Dance; which will contain no Jazz rhythm, no rhythm from the waist down; but from the solar plexus, the temporal home of the soul, upwards to the Star-Spangled Banner of the sky which arches over that great stretch of land from the Pacific, over the Plains, over the Sierra Nevadas, over the Rocky Mountains to the Atlantic."[5]

A second American movement was initiated—also about

FIGURE 39. Ruth Dennis as Radha (United States, 1906)

1904—by Ruth Dennis (stage name, Ruth St. Denis), a musical comedy and vaudeville dancer who had likewise turned her back on the ballet. The popular cigarette brands of that decade were Egyptian Deities and Rameses II, and the picture of a goddess on one of the ads inspired her to an imitation. Moreover, ever since the appearance in yellow robe and turban of the handsome Swami Vivekananda, in September 1893, at the great World Parliament of Religions, held in Chicago in connection with the Columbian Exposition of that year, there had been a scent in the American air, not only of Turkish tobacco, but also of oriental incense, and Miss Ruth (as she was later affectionately called), turning from one directly to the other, composed in 1906 her famous signature piece, *Radha*, which accompanied her on a European tour from 1906 to 1909. Ted Shawn, meanwhile, a former divinity student, had been introduced to dance as therapy following an illness, and in 1914 he and Ruth

St. Denis met. They married and together formed the crucial Denishawn Company, out of which there were to come three of the major creative dancers of the following generation: Martha Graham, who was a member of the company from 1916 to 1923; Doris Humphrey, from 1918 to 1928; and Charles Weidman, who had been brought into the fold by Humphrey.

The dances of this Denishawn School were rather picturesque than formal, theatrical than technical. Although there was an interest in ethnic sources, little attention was paid to the grounding principles of any of the adopted styles. Ted Shawn described their approach to composition as proceeding in four stages. There was, first, the idea; second, the bodily movement; third, the "tonalizing" of the movement in terms of music; and fourth, the costuming and scenery.[6]

In relation to step three, there was the practice termed "music visualization," which had been derived—like the personal art of the young Japanese Michio Ito—from a Dalcroze inspiration. Neither St. Denis nor Shawn had ever worked directly—as Ito had—with Émile Jaques-Dalcroze himself, but knowledge of the basic idea and practice of his system of eurythmics now was general: the practice, namely, of patterning bodily movements on musical rhythms. In large group compositions this might involve the assignment of one dancer to the interpretation of each instrument in the orchestra. The movements so assigned in a Denishawn production, however, were not based, like those of Ito's compositions, on the architectural order of a consistent dance vocabulary systematically developed out of an aesthetic theory. On the contrary, like the scenery and costuming, they were based on imitations of the forms of the exotic culture. The extraordinary success of St. Denis and Shawn's performances in both Europe and America suggests that there must have been throughout the Western world in that period of an approaching First World War a longing—or at least readiness—for a breakaway from the already tightening iron ring of the Machine Age and its associated philosophies of British Utilitarianism, North

American Pragmatism, French Positivism, German Socialism, and a mechanistic view of science. An aroma of temple incense seemed to emanate from their dances, telling of a time and of distant lands where mythology and prayer (not science and sociology) were the inspiration of art. In New York City, in 1875, the Russian-born Mme. Helena Blavatsky had founded the mystically inspired Theosophical Society, which in the following decades rapidly spread, establishing centers not only throughout Europe and America, but in India as well. And there is in Ruth St. Denis's art an unmistakable suggestion of the influence of this movement in her recognition of a common ground of mystical realization informing the arts and civilizations of both Antiquity and the Orient. Ted Shawn, the former divinity student who had himself experienced the healing power of dance, must also, as her partner and spouse, have contributed to her appreciation of the hermetic dimension of this most ancient of the arts. However, the accent in the Denishawn productions on the exotic ethnic features of the imitated forms tended rather to fix the mind on their remote, historically conditioned, regional associations, than to fulfill the first condition of art as formulated by the poet Yeats,[7] which is, namely, "the disengagement of a soul from place and history."

The same might, of course, be said of the effect of the Greek costumes of Isadora; for to her audiences, at least, these suggested an imitation. The fact, furthermore, that her brother Raymond and a number of the members of his Paris school habitually appeared in Greek costume on the city's streets—like Platonic ideas incarnate—suggests that the posture must, indeed, have been in some way seriously intended. And in the late 1930s, when Raymond, so costumed, stepped out of a train in the New York Sixth Avenue subway, the incongruity of the mythological identification smote the eye.[8]

However, in dance there is something else besides costume and setting to be recognized, which to the historian (and, hence,

FIGURE 40. Raymond Duncan with his wife and child (France, 1912)

to the records of this ephemeral art) must remain, and can only forever remain, unknown—which is to say, the *dancer*: the elegance of the bodily form, grace, flow, and timing of each gesture! In James Joyce's words, the beheld "relation of part to part, of each part to the whole, and of the whole to each of its parts,"[9] in the immediate being and moment of the dancer and dance, on stage.

Undoubtedly, it was affectively the bodily presences of these two beautiful women themselves in movement that electrified their audiences, and whatever theories may have inspired them to their dances have to be judged, in relation to the actual events, merely as invisible backgrounds to unduplicable aesthetic effects beyond time.

In relation to their effects on our Western theatrical arts, on the other hand, the careers of these two Americans marked the opening of a modern era. Their breakaway from the ballet was but the prelude to complementary courses: one representing a living image of enraptured spontaneity, Greek in its inspiration, earthly and physical in its beauty; the other archaic and oriental, suggesting through its physical beauty, overtones of a spiritual, astral order, known to mankind from Antiquity, lost today to the West, but preserved in the mysterious East.

CHAPTER 8

———————●———————

IN A WIDELY PUBLISHED ESSAY entitled "The Philosopher's Stone of Dancing," Isadora Duncan wrote the following:

> In music, there are three sorts of composers: first, those who think out a scholarly music, who seek about and arrange, through their brains, a skillful and subtly effective score which appeals through the mind to the senses. Second, there are those who know how to translate their own emotions into the medium of sound, the joys and sorrows of their own hearts creating a music that appeals directly to the listener's heart, and brings tears by the memories it evokes of joys and sorrows, by the remembrance of happiness gone by. Third, there are those who, subconsciously, hear with their souls some melody of another world, and are able to express this in terms comprehensible and joyous to human ears.
>
> There are likewise three kinds of dancers: first, those who consider dancing as a sort of gymnastic drill, made up of impersonal and graceful arabesques; second, those who, by concentrating their minds, lead the body into the rhythm of a desired emotion, expressing a remembered feeling or experience. And finally, there are those who convert the body into a luminous fluidity, surrendering it to the inspiration of the soul. This third sort of dancer understands that the body, by force of the soul, can in fact be converted to a luminous fluid. The flesh becomes light and transparent, as shown through the X-ray—but with the difference that the human soul is lighter than these rays. When, in its divine power, it completely possesses the body, it converts that into a luminous moving cloud and thus can manifest itself in the whole of its divinity. This is the explanation of the miracle of St. Francis walking on the sea.. His

body no longer weighed like ours, so light had it become through the soul.

Imagine then a dancer who, after long study, prayer, and inspiration, has attained such a degree of understanding that his body is simply the luminous manifestation of his soul; whose body dances in accordance with a music heard inwardly, in an expression of something out of another, a profounder world. This is the truly creative dancer, natural but not imitative, speaking in movement out of himself and out of something greater than all selves.

FIGURE 41. *Isadora Duncan* by Abraham Walkowitz (watercolor and ink on paper, United States, 1915)

So confident am I that the soul can be awakened, can completely possess the body, that when I have taken children into my schools I have aimed above all else to bring to them a consciousness of this power within themselves, of their relationship to the universal rhythm, to evoke from them the ecstasy, the beauty of this realization. The means to this awakening may be in part a revelation of the beauty of nature, and it may be in part that sort of music that the third group of composers gives us, that arises from and speaks to the soul.

There are perhaps grown people who have forgotten the language of the soul. But children understand. It is only necessary to say to them: "Listen to the music with your soul. Now, while you are listening, do you not feel an inner self awakening deep within you that it is by its strength that your head is lifted, that your arms are raised, that you are walking slowly toward the light?"

This awakening is the first step in dancing, as I understand it.

When I began to dance with the movements and gestures that my enraptured soul knew how to communicate to my body, others began to imitate me, not understanding that it was necessary to go back to a beginning, to find something in themselves first. In many theatres and schools I have seen these dancers, who comprehended only with the brain, who loaded down their dances with gestures; and their movements seemed empty, dull and devoid of meaning. What they translated through the mind lacked all inspiration, all life. So, too, do those systems of dancing that are only arranged gymnastics, only too logically understood (Dalcroze, etc.). It seems to me criminal to entrust children, who cannot defend themselves, to this injurious training; for it is a crime to teach the child to guide his growing body by the stern power of the brain, while deadening impulse and inspiration.

The only power that can satisfactorily guide the child's body is the inspiration of the soul.[1]

Isadora's sister-in-law, Margharita Duncan, has left us a description of a moment in 1911 when she illustrated to her pupils in an unforgettable way the leading principle of her mastery:

She had been teaching them the dance of the Happy Spirits in her *Orpheus* program. After they had learned the gestures and the groupings, there came a day when that was not enough and she spoke to them something like this:

"Don't be merely graceful. Nobody is interested in a lot of graceful young girls. Unless your dancing springs from an inner emotion and expresses an idea, it will be meaningless and the audience will be bored. I'll show you the difference. First I will dance the music in the way I want you to dance it, then in the way I want you to avoid."

Whereupon she performed one of her marvels of apparent simplicity; a little skipping, a few upward and outward gestures of the head and arms, and heavenly beauty was created, the serene joy of the Blessed Spirits filled the studio. Then she executed the same movements, with no perceptible variation, but in such a merely graceful manner that I was astonished at the different result. I would not have believed that she could make a dance look like that. And she was not exaggerating her effect by any least simper of face or body. She was simply leaving out the animating spirit, and what was left, unbelievable as it may sound, was, as she said, entirely uninteresting. Except as an object lesson.[2]

CHAPTER 9

———————•———————

OSWALD SPENGLER in *The Decline of the West* distinguishes in the production of an artwork two factors, representing contrasting aspects of our living. One, which he describes as grounded in our genes and the current of life that pulses in our veins, he terms the Totem or Totemic factor. The other, which is a product of our waking-consciousness—nerves, brains, and eyes—he terms Taboo, as representing a fixing, binding, and controlling force. The Taboo side of an art is represented in its stock of forms, conventions, and specific technical disciplines, which can be taught and constitute its language. That which is Totem, on the other hand, cannot be taught, but only awakened; for it is inherited and innate. In Spengler's own words:

> Totem and Taboo describe the ultimate meanings of Being and Waking Being, Destiny and Causality, Race and Language, Time and Space, yearning and fear, pulse and tension.... The Totem side of life is plantlike and inheres in all being, while the Taboo side is animal and presupposes the free movement of a being in the world. Our Totem organs are those of the blood-circulation and of reproduction, our Taboo organs those of the senses and the nerves. All that is of Totem has physiognomy, all that is of Taboo has system. In the Totemistic resides the common feeling of beings that belong to the same stream of existence. It cannot be acquired and cannot be got rid of; it is a fact, the fact of all facts. That which is of Taboo, on the other hand, is the characteristic of linkages of waking-consciousness, it is learnable and acquirable, and on that

very account guarded as a secret by cult-communities, philosophers' schools, and artists' guilds each of which possesses a sort of
cryptic language of its own.[1]

In the cult language of the modern movement, these two
components of the action of a dance are known as dynamics and
shape, the vocabulary of any established style being the product
of a union of the two. Where either is lacking in the execution of
a work, there is no dance—as Isadora demonstrated to her class
on the occasion just described.

Indeed, it might be said that her own great art was all Totem. It commenced inward, in the rapture of an idea, and moved
outward into space. Hence her absolute rejection of every impo-
sition of structuring form from without; not only the unnatural,
athletic stunts of ballet, but also the conceptually patterned imitations of musical scores in the Dalcroze system of eurythmics.
Her own responses to the inspiration of music were not in that
way literally patterned to the score, but were released from what
she called her soul by immediate experiences of the orchestra.
She tells, for example, of her joy in dancing to the baton of
Walter Damrosch:

> How can I describe the joy of dancing with this orchestra? It is
> there before me—Walter Damrosch raises his baton—I watch it,
> and, at the first stroke there surges within me the combined sym-
> phonic chord of all the instruments in one. The mighty reverber-
> ation rushes over me and I become the medium to condense in
> unified expression the joy of Brunnhilde awakened by Siegfried,
> or the soul of Isolde seeking in Death her realization. Voluminous,
> vast, swelling like sails in the wind, the movements of my dance
> carry me onward—onward and upward; and I feel the presence of
> a mighty power within me which listens to the music and then
> reaches out through all my body, trying to find an outlet for this
> listening. Sometimes this power grew furious, sometimes it raged
> and shook me until my heart nearly burst from its passion, and
> I thought my last moments on earth had surely arrived. At other
> times it brooded heavily, and I would suddenly feel such anguish
> that, through my arms stretched to the Heavens, I implored help
> from where no help came. Often I thought to myself, what a mis-
> take to call me a dancer—I am the magnetic center to convey the

emotional expression of the Orchestra. From my soul sprang fiery rays to connect me with my trembling vibrating Orchestra.

There was a flutist who played so divinely the solo of the Happy Souls in *Orpheus* that I often found myself immobile on the stage, with the tears flowing from my eyes, just from the ecstasy of listening to him, and the singing of the violins and the whole orchestra soaring upwards, inspired by the wonderful conductor.

There was a marvelous sympathy between Damrosch and me, and to each one of his gestures, I instantly felt the answering vibration. As he augmented the crescendo in volume, so the life in me mounted and overflowed in gesture—for each musical phrase translated into a musical movement, my whole being vibrated in harmony with his.[2]

The introduction into the studios of the modern American dance of an appreciation of the structuring Taboo side of the art was the effect, chiefly, of two influences: first, the arrival in New York in 1916 of the Japanese Michio Ito, and then, through four decades, the lifetime teaching of Louis Horst, until the year of his death at the age of eighty in 1964.

FIGURE 42. Michio Ito in *Bushido* (United States, 1916)

The arrival of Ito was sensational. On November 13, 1916, the Washington Square Players presented a Kabuki play, *Bushido*, in English, with Michio Ito, the poet Yeats's young friend, as both scene designer and codirector. Katharine Cornell made her professional debut in this production, and in the *New York Times*, Alexander Woollcott wrote of it:

> Every once in a blue moon a playwright or a player achieves a
> moment of dramatic suspense so intense that the theater grows still
> as death and your heart stops beating. Such a moment is the climax
> of *Bushido*, itself the climax of the most successful program in the
> history of the Washington Square Players.[3]

Until 1929, Ito remained then in New York, composing, performing, teaching, directing, and producing. In 1919 he appeared in John Murray Anderson's *Greenwich Village Follies*, and in 1922 he composed and directed a revue of his own: *Michio Ito's Pinwheel Revel*. The year 1927 saw his name as choreographer of a Shubert production of *Cherry Blossoms*, Winthrop Ames's production of *The Mikado*, and the American Opera Company's *Madame Butterfly*, for which his brother Yuji Ito designed and executed the costumes. In March 1928 he directed the League of Composers' presentation of Igor Stravinsky's *L'Histoire du soldat*; in May, took part, along with Martha Graham and Benjamin Zemach, in a performance of three "orchestral dramas" to the music of Debussy, presented with the Cleveland Symphony Orchestra at the Metropolitan Opera House; and in 1929 he departed for Los Angeles on a U.S. tour with his own dance group, of which Georgia Graham (Martha Graham's sister) was a member.

It is not easy to measure the impact upon the native American constellation of the brilliance and teaching of this scion of Japan, by way of Dalcroze, W. B. Yeats, and Ezra Pound. Angna Enters, Georgia Graham, Pauline Koner, and Lester Horton were among the number of his dancers, and that Martha Graham owed some debt to him as well is evident from the fact, at least, that it was he who introduced her one day in John Murray

Anderson's Broadway studio to the sculptor Isamu Noguchi, who later became her set designer. Ted Shawn wrote of him in those years that he was "constantly presenting premiers of new works...: at one time he took a Broadway theater and presented full evenings of dance with many guest artists from the contemporary American dance field, and provided the friendly environment to develop much new and valuable talent—Angna Enters made some of her first appearances in Michio Ito's *Pinwheel*." And Shawn states of him, also, in summary: "Ito, a Japanese, was truly one of the American modern dance pioneers."[4]

It would be hard to think of an ideal of art more radically in contrast to the antiformal, inspirational approach of Isadora Duncan than that of traditional Japan, where it is precisely from the Taboo side that all learning disciplines take off. Indeed, the whole of life there is of this order. The learning method is of practice, practice, according to the precise models of one or another of the schools until accurate action becomes automatic. The creative act is given life then by the impulse of an experienced idea, of which the required accurate action is as a gesture. So, too, of course, in the ballet! One can understand, therefore, why Michio Ito's notion of his architecturally structured vocabulary of dance was that it was an occidental, not Japanese, sort of ballet, constructed on the European base of Jaques-Dalcroze's eurythmics. In his view, the background of Japanese dancing is literary; that of Western dancing, music. In both, the performer is a medium of thought and emotion, the energy-charged idea; but in the Western art, since it is the more abstract, the spectator is left free to his own imagination, whereas in a dance composed to poetry or prose, the reference is specific and already given in words.

"When I dance," Ito is reported to have declared, "the music does not accompany me.... We become as one. Sometimes the instrument has the melody, sometimes I have it, and sometimes the melodies are intertwined."[5]

In Ito's opinion, according to his pupil Helen Caldwell,

the highest realization of his own abstract art was in the great choreographic symphonies that he composed in California: his Pageant of Lights, for example, which celebrated the opening of the Pasadena Rose Bowl, September 20, 1929, with 180 dancers accompanied by the Hollywood Symphony Orchestra, performing to Grieg, Dvořák, Tchaikovsky, and Chopin, against a golden backdrop-screen, 40 feet high and 125 feet long. As Caldwell states of his art in this period of his apogee: while still true to the Dalcroze idea of musical visualization, it surpassed anything he had accomplished in New York; for in these choreographies "there was no pantomime or realistic representation of any sort to distract the mind from the music's charm; as always with Ito, music and dance were at one."[6]

A second, even more gorgeous, American folk event was presented, again at the Hollywood Bowl, August 15, 1930, to an audience of some twenty thousand. Even while in a small Greek-style theater on the Argus estate at Eagle Rock, members of his master classes were performing in a series of intimate Monday evening recitals—before elite audiences of intellectuals and artists, such as would have pleased the poet Yeats himself—*At the Hawk's Well* and two Japanese *kyōgen*.

Michio Ito remained in Hollywood thirteen years, continuing in full career until the crisis of Pearl Harbor, when he returned to Japan, to open there a studio that is still in operation, continuing to produce and teach until his death, November 6, 1961.

The second and finally more substantially influential figure in the introduction to the studios of the developing modern American dance of a respect for the Taboo side of the art was Louis Horst. As musical director of the Denishawn Dancers from 1915 to 1925, it was he who encouraged Martha Graham, Doris Humphrey, and Charles Weidman to develop their own styles. And after leaving Denishawn in association with Graham to become the pianist, director, and constant mentor of her company, he turned his mind, also, for the next four decades to the larger task of educating the entire American dance community in the forms and history of choreography in the West. He served in this teaching role on the staffs of many of the most notable American schools of modern dance: the Neighborhood Playhouse School of Theatre in New York City, 1928 to 1948; the Bennington College Summer School of Dance from 1934 to 1945, and from 1948 to 1953; the Connecticut College Summer School, to which the Bennington project had been transferred; in New York City, following his turn at the Neighborhood Playhouse, he taught from 1948 to 1951 at the Jean Erdman Theater of Dance; and from 1951 to 1964 at the Juilliard School of Music. Horst's emphasis throughout was, first, on the principles of musical structure: not the following of note patterns in the way of a eurythmic visualization of a score already composed, nor the opening of the body and mind to the impacts of an already known orchestral work, with enactments, then, of the rapture; but an elementary, methodical learning of the fundamentals of musical organization, so that new dance compositions, independently structured according to tested laws, might be conceived and produced—to which end he published, as teaching texts, *Pre-classic Dance Forms* (1937) and *Modern Dance Forms* (1961). A related concern was the development in his students of an appreciation for the visual, stylistic values of the art, and he would propose, therefore, for emulation, models from various stylistic periods of the Western visual arts, as inspirations for their own exercises in the shaping of new works. In 1933 Horst founded a monthly magazine, the *Dance Observer*, which became and remained until 1964, the year of his death at the age of eighty, the pedagogical master and sole fostering medium of the modern movement in those precious formative years of its coming into being.[7] He also accompanied the concerts and composed scores to many of the compositions of his friends and protégés, who included, among others, Martha Graham, Doris Humphrey, Helen Tamiris, Jean Erdman, and Charles Weidman.

CHAPTER IO

In Germany, meanwhile, Rudolf von Laban (1879–1958) had been developing a system for the recording of human motion now known as Labanotation,[1] which is based on a recognition of the relationship of the body's structure to its capacity for motion and direction. As a Taboo system (in Spengler's sense), Labanotation is not something to be imposed upon the dancer as a discipline from without. On the contrary: it functions as a clarification and mapping of all the possibilities of exteriorization and extension-into-space of any impulse. Taking the natural, dynamic urge of the body to motion to be the force that impels the performer to a rhythmic self-discharge, its formulas designate twelve primary directions of possible extension of the impulse into space—the aesthetic implication being that, as dance, the motion will be authentic, and hence significant, only in so far as it is an extension undeformed of the artist's inner life.[2] It is thus a theory of motion and a system of recording that perfectly accords with the position of Isadora Duncan, as also, indeed, with the whole Romantic, Germanic tradition represented in the three great names that she recognized as her European Masters: Beethoven, Wagner, and Nietzsche. Mary Wigman, who would go on to found the German school of the Modern Dance movement, studied with Laban, first in Munich and then, following

FIGURE 43. Rudolf von Laban demonstrating Labanotation (Germany, 1929)

the opening of the war, at the Choreographic Institute, which he founded in Zurich in 1915. Wigman had commenced her studies in 1911 at the Dalcroze School in Hellerau—the year that Michio Ito arrived, when she was twenty-five, and he eighteen. The season in Zurich was contemporary with the labors in that delightful little city of James Joyce on *Ulysses*, Hugo Ball and Tristan Tzara on the invention of Dada in the Cabaret Voltaire, and Carl G. Jung on his theories of "psychological types" and "archetypes of the unconscious." Already in 1919 Wigman was giving her first solo performances in Switzerland and Germany, having composed in 1914 the first version of her celebrated, masked *Witch Dance*, as well as *Lento* and *A Day of Elves*; in 1917, *The Tumbler of Our Lady*; and in 1918–19, four *Ecstatic Dances* (Prayer, Sacrifice, Idolatry, and Temple Dance), *Four Hungarian Dances* (based on Brahms), *Eroica*, *Waltz*, and a *Marche Orientale* (in three movements). In 1920 she founded in

FIGURE 44. Mary Wigman (Germany, 1922)

Dresden the Central Institute of all the later Wigman Schools, and in 1922 performed with a small "chamber group" in Berlin.

Already in her titles—*Witch Dance, A Day of Elves, Tumbler of Our Lady,* and *Ecstatic Dances* (Prayer, Sacrifice, Idolatry, and Temple Dance)—an interest is indicated in mythological inspiration, while in her account of the manner in which the second version of her *Witch Dance* was composed in 1926, her understanding of the relationship of mythic to psychological imagery and dynamics is vividly evident.

As she tells it:

While cleaning a closet in my school, I found an old worn piece of brocade. It had served generations of my students for costume studies, and it showed all the traces of its final disintegration. I was at the point of destroying it when I suddenly remembered what this fabric once was: the costume for the *Witch Dance*, which belonged to one of the "great" solos of my career. I saw myself standing in a Swiss silk store and staring in fascination at this splendor spread out before me: bold designs in metal threads on a copper-red background shimmering in gold and silver traced in black—exciting, wild, barbaric. I was as if hypnotized and bought the fabric against my better judgment. It was outrageously expensive, and I knew only too well that I had no use for it. I had a bad conscience, and thus this piece of splendor went into the fabric drawer of my costume closet where it remained hidden from my eyes for years. I created new solo and group dances, the various characters of *Visions*[3] grew into being.

The creative urge got hold of me again. What its intention was, where it would lead me, was not yet clearly recognizable. Only the restlessness was there, and some kind of evil greed that I felt in my hands, which pressed themselves clawlike into the ground as if they wanted to take root. I had the sensation of being full to the point of bursting and near desperation, I felt it ought to be possible to give shape to whatever it was that distressed me beyond measure.

Sometimes at night I slipped into the studio and worked myself up into a rhythmic intoxication in order to come closer to the slowly stirring character. I could feel how everything pointed toward a clearly defined dance figure. The richness of rhythmic ideas was overwhelming. But something was opposed to their becoming lucid and orderly, something that forced my body time and again into a sitting or squatting position in which the greedy hands could take possession of the ground.

When, one night, I returned to my room utterly agitated, I looked into the mirror by chance. What it reflected was the image of one possessed, wild and dissolute, repelling and fascinating. The hair unkempt, the eyes deep in their sockets, the nightgown shifted about, which made the body appear almost shapeless: there she was—the witch—the earth-bound creature with her unrestrained, naked instincts, with her insatiable lust for life, beast and woman at one and the same time.

I shuddered at my own image, at the exposure of this facet of my ego which I had never allowed to emerge in such unashamed nakedness. But, after all, isn't a bit of the witch hidden in every hundred percent female, no matter what form its origin may have?

FIGURE 45. *Totentanz der Mary Wigman* by Ernst Ludwig Kirchner (paint on canvas, Germany, c. 1926–28)

All that had to be done was to tame this elemental creature, to mold her and to work on one's own body as on a sculpture. It was wonderful to abandon oneself to the craving for evil, to imbibe the powers which usually dared to stir only weakly beneath one's civilized surface. But all this had to be surrendered to the rules of creation, the rules which had to be based on the essence and character of the dance-shape itself, to define and reflect it truly once and for all. I had to take this into consideration and to be extremely careful, so that the creative urge should be neither weakened nor blocked in the process of molding and shaping.

Does not the power, the magnificence of all creative art lie in knowing how to force chaos into form? A form which as an idea, as symbol, and as simile becomes, so to speak, second nature, to prove itself on a higher level as a work of art? The artistic form is not an end in itself, is not being created to turn numb and torpid the fermenting matter from which it arises. It is the receptacle which, time and again, grows hot with, and is inflamed by, the living content, until the mutual melting-down process is fully completed, and from this point on only the artistic action speaks to us. My witch figure also had to be brought to the point of this entity and had to receive her profile in an outward and plastic manifestation that was hers. The scales fell from my eyes: the piece of brocade! Did it not possess, in its barbaric beauty, in its splendiferous ruthlessness, something that corresponded to the revolting character of the dance? And there was still left the first and never used mask of the Ceremonial Figure,[4] whose features were my own translated into the demonic.

I suddenly knew that fabric and mask belonged together and that they had had to wait this long for their return from exile in order that, as costume and mask, they might give the *Witch Dance* its representative, its very own stage image. The creation of the dance went faster than I had imagined. The discovered motifs fell into place in an unbroken chain and stood up to the demands of the composition. Only the mask caused some headache. In contrast to the mask finally used in the *Ceremonial Figure*, which preserved its immaculate, expressive smoothness through all phases of the dance, also in contrast to the frightening masked figures of the *Dance of Death*, which was later created as a group dance,[5] the *Witch Dance* mask possessed its own personal life. Every movement of the body evoked or changed expression of the face; depending on the position of the head the eyes seemed to close or to open. As a matter of fact, even around the mouth—intimated with a few strokes of the brush—there seemed to play a smile which, in its unfathomableness, was reminiscent of the Sphinx. The body, too, burdened with heaviness, possessed something of the lurking, animal-like quality in the image of the enigmatic Sphinx, even though only by way of intimation.

"Keep the secret…" What a discovery! By incorporating this element, which became clarified through the warning gesture covering the mouth, through the play of question and answer between a remote background plunged into twilight and the glaring foreground action, the character of the dance, tumultuous in itself, found its corresponding opposite pole, for which I had searched in vain for a long time. Only now *Witch Dance* was really accomplished.

I believe that *Witch Dance* was the only one among my solo dances that did not make me shake with stage fright before every performance. How I loved it, this growing into the excitement of its expressive world, how intensely I tried in each performance to feel myself back into the original creative condition of *Witch Dance* and to fulfill its stirring form by returning to the very point where it all began.[6]

FIGURE 46. *Dancing Mary Wigman* by Ernst Ludwig Kirchner (paint on canvas, Germany, 1933)

In the masked dance *Totenmal*—"Memorial to the Dead" composed in 1930 in memory of the dead of World War I—a stunning conjunction of the aesthetic, mythic, and psychological orders of attention was achieved.

Wigman herself declared:

So far this work was probably the most mature and inventive of all my group compositions. It was built symphonically throughout as pure dance, based on no connected action. Its three movements— solemn, sombre, exalted—differed only in their essential mood and contrasted in their spatial and creative forces. The first movement—called "Temple" in the program bill—consisted of four dances following one another in immediate sequence, dances whose monotonous character was based on a movement pattern in harmony with its solemn message—a kind of "ostinato" which received in each dance another nuance, another tempo, a new variation of its basic rhythm. It was a fourfold paraphrasing of a theme which, in its totality, achieved the effect of a celebration characteristic of a cult. The solemnity was still retained in the ecstatic whirl of my *Monotony*: for here I cast myself as a soloist, a single voice weaving through the whole fabric like a red thread, binding it together.

The sombre movement, *In the Sign of the Dark*, was totally attuned to the rhythmic-dynamic element. Sharply profiled groups, whose tight structure gave an almost architectonic impression, were brought to spatial solution, as were the constantly mounting tensions, through the exploitation of overrefined footwork. The diagonal principle dominated space and was linked—in the straddled leg attitude in its forward movement with knife-sharp rhythms of the feet, thrust high in a vertical direction by the grouping: now tearing space open, creating abysses, now filling space, towering high, only to burst it open again. It was contrapuntally built to flow into a theme composed like a fugue and to find its conclusion in total space harmony.

The costumes of the dancers corresponded with the dramatic structure arrested in its ominous darkness: a dull black, steelgray brocade, glistening silver, and, as the only color spot, a dark-glowing burgundy red. Those were the colors. The cut of the costumes: knee-length mantles falling in wide folds from the shoulder, underlining the horizontal pattern of movement. And opposed to it were the vertically stressed figures in tight dresses barely hidden by the narrow long mantle opening in front.

To this very day I have not forgotten how impressively the dance action unfolded in its sparse color, in its almost Spartan austerity, before a deep blue cyclorama draped black on both sides. And hardly ever again did I succeed in creating such absolute harmony of color, form, and line of physical and spatial rhythms as in this work.

Festive Finale, the third and last movement, was introduced by five dancers carrying cymbals and going to their places in sharp turns on a zigzag way. They stood there like pillars, dividing the space asymmetrically in order to introduce the festive action with the rhythmic motif of their metallic-sounding instruments. They formed, so to speak, static moments in the light-footed airiness of movement to and fro which permeated the dance space they created, the dancers winding around them garlandlike, circling and turning, leaping and swinging, in an exciting up and down of swaying vibrato which was heightened by a jubilant crescendo.

But at the beginning of each new thematic phase the static figures moved to another position, from which they ushered in the return of the varied movement sequences with the motif of their quickly repeated beats of the cymbals. How happy I was with this

idea!... Three times this change took place which, in the crescendo
of its last phase, was whipped up to a fortissimo and then followed,
while gradually fading out, by a pastoral theme. Rows, curves, arcs,
and circles glidingly fell apart and again united in the kneeling,
sitting, and reclining dancers into loosely formed groups. Only a
few figures emerged from it in order to surrender to the now fully
widened space in fleeting encounters, in the gentle rocking of the
bodies, in the lightly moving play of hands. It was the quiet after
the storm, in which the static figures were also a part. Then once
more the call of the beating cymbals sounded. Once more the space
turned into the column-formed dance area, to find its festive finale
in harmony with the great jubilation of *Celebration.*

FIGURE 47. *Totenmal* (Germany, c. 1930)

In the scenes of *Totenmal,* two choruses opposed each other: lov-
ing women who in the torment of their loneliness advanced to the
threshold of death, obsessed by the mad notion they could obliter-
ate the finality of separation and recall the beloved in his former
shape. And opposed to them the phantomlike male chorus symbol-
izing the dead of the war, appearing bigger than life—in staring
silence, in painful, passive defense, and finally in rebellion against
the women's invasion into the shadowy, twilight abode which it
was no longer in their power to leave.

Now it certainly lies within the scope of the dance to give profile and shape to the transcendental; but here I encountered fully
unexpected difficulties, inhibitions which arose within me. For it
was no longer a matter of conjuring up the ghostlike as such. Dignity had to be preserved, awe before the majesty of death, who, even
in his most incomprehensible action remains the unimpeachable
keeper of the seal within his realm.

Fear, horror, terror, pain, and despair of death—the experience
of the women was burdened with all these images of war, while the
male chorus stood in the realm of the forlorn and forgotten, never
again to be reached by anything. There was no longer any love nor
the understanding of human demands. And yet it did not suffice to
force the male chorus onto a level where it would remain merely an
apparition. In spite of all remoteness, in spite of the chorus being
taken back into a schematic and shadowlike existence, it had to get
into action, had to become the antagonist.

Time and again I could not succeed in balancing reality and
superreality. Until one day I remembered the song of the Odyssey
in which the great wanderer performs the expiation and blood sacrifice in order to meet the shadowy souls of the dominion of death,
and, in conversation with them, to compensate for the loss of his
past, suffered through his long wandering. I virtually saw how the
shapeless shadows, while in touch with the blood still warm with
life, regained the intimation of their human features—how they
became recognizable, how one could address them, yet how they
remained untouchable. And though this vision could not be immediately exploited, it nevertheless kindled a little light with whose
help I dared to grope forward into the inaccessible unknown.

With the exception of a single figure—a part in which I cast
myself—all *Totenmal* dancers were supposed to wear masks. Con-
founded, I stood in front of the fifty faces carved in wood. Could
they be adjusted to the abstracting process of a dance creation?
In the broad surface treatment of the wood, in the expression of
the painfully stern defense and retreat, the male masks could be
best adjusted to an almost ghostlike message. On the other hand,
the torn-open faces of the women were brought into a focus of
too much realism, which—even though on a different level—also
seemed to be forced into something phantomlike. And thus the
first practical attempt failed by falling somewhat into the grotesque.
What was to be done? I knew no way out. And yet a way had to be
found to come closer to these masks.

We tried it with "meditation exercises." The female dancers sat on the floor with their backs to the wall and stared at the masks lying in their laps: one minute—two minutes—five minutes. No word was spoken. Only a softly playing gong melody filled the room. The same was done next evening. But that time the dancers had put the masks on their faces and observed them as reflections in mirrors which they had brought with them. This way we gradually adopted and became immersed in the style and character of the masks.

Then I began with the molding of each single figure. I had every dancer approach the large mirror in my studio in order to show where the discrepancy could be found between mask and human shape. I particularly remember the dancer wearing the mask of an old woman. Her body was in utter contrast to the tormented face of the mask, furrowed with wrinkles and with the expression of one about to die. Only with utter cautiousness did I then succeed in giving the young body the gait, posture, and gesture, the imprint of the decrepitude of old age. It was an endlessly troublesome, detailed job during which I was concerned not only with bringing mask and mask-wearer into harmony with each other, but also with determining their style and with turning them into types while preserving their individual character. Only in this way could the collaboration of all in the choric message be achieved....[7]

The ideal in mind had been to create a piece, not simply of dance, but a work of Total Theater, a *Gesamtkunstwerk*, whose total effect one could not escape; and indeed, as Wigman recalled: "Night after night the huge festival hall especially built for *Totenmal* was filled with people who were deeply stirred. There were those awe-inspiring moments in which, from the galleries, a few speakers read letters written by students killed in the war. Moments in which one sat there with bated breath, and soundless weeping seemed to fill the auditorium."[8]

The dance that had come into being as a preliminary study for this great work was a visionary solo, called *Space Shape*. As Wigman tells it:

It was physically so strenuous that I could take it into my solo program for only a short period of years. A double strip of fabric consisting of red silk and silver-grey velvet was worked into the wide skirt of my dance costume. This strip was about thirteen feet long and fastened on its other end to a hollow wooden stick filled with lead which lay heavily in my hands. Only this made it possible to cope with the unusual material and to master it dancewise—to throw and to swing it far through the air, to whirl it so tightly around the body that it turned into a pillar, and to unfold it again in a far-reaching low movement thus, winglike, throwing the air-and-floor-space into tumult. It was a man's job which, basically, went far beyond my strength, but which put me into a position of conveying to the dancers of *Totenmal* the execution of their task in a competent and expert manner. It would have been easy to let the last scene of *Totenmal* turn into a hellish pandemonium, into a raid of a too theatrically exploited underworld throwing itself with hatred against an animated reality and overrunning it with blind fury. But this was just what it should not be. The criterion for all the other scenes had to be applied here too: to be a memorial for the dead of the war, erected in a consecrated hour, a memento for the living and the survivors too.[9]

The method of teaching in the schools of Mary Wigman's art was based substantially on the movement studies of Laban, with an emphasis, not on choreography, but on a systematic exploration of the possibilities of the instrument: the body and its resources. Class problems in selected aspects of the principles of movement; daily exercises in improvisation, movement—discovery and—combination; the progressive isolation of elements to be practiced, which when combined made up a kind of anatomy of movement: these placed the emphasis of instruction, not on the visual image of the teacher as model, but on a cognized image of the dancer's own anatomy as an instrument for the translation of impulse into action.

In 1930 and 1931, Mary Wigman, with her company, toured the United States, leaving Hanya Holm to establish and direct in New York the only authentic Wigman School in America. The Denishawn Company had by that time broken up, and Michio Ito was in California. Louis Horst and Martha Graham had established in the city a school of modern dance of their own, as likewise had Doris Humphrey and Charles Weidman. Holm, therefore—who had commenced her career as a teacher

FIGURE 48. Hanya Holm (England, 1958)

of the Dalcroze Method, and after entering the Wigman School in Dresden became a leading member of the Concert Group as well as of the board of directors of the Wigman Central Institute—soon found herself, in both her teaching and her dance, representing a point of view in evident contrast to that of the two young American studios out of Denishawn. As she herself wrote of this in a statement published in 1935:

> Soon after the beginning of my work here I found myself moved by certain differences in environment and temperament which came gradually, if not to change, at least to color my former convictions and attitudes. As time passed I tried to clarify and analyze these differences and to seek for that unity without which the ideals of the dance education as conceived by Mary Wigman could have no real part in the field of the American dance....
>
> The entire orientation of the dance of Mary Wigman is towards the establishment of a relationship between man and his universe. It

is this philosophical tendency that influences the emotional, spatial, and functional aspects of her own dancing and likewise her pedagogical principles. Emotionally the German dance is basically subjective and the American dance objective in their characteristic manifestations. This is of course a generalization and as such true only to the point of the exceptions, but I believe it throws some light on their fundamental emotional departures. The tendency of the American dancer is to observe, portray, and comment on her surroundings with an insight lighted mainly by intellectual comprehension and analysis....The German dancer on the other hand starts with the actual emotional experience itself and its effect upon the individual. The distinction is one of "being" as contrasted with "doing"—of immersing the self in an emotional state as the necessary prelude to creation as contrasted with the objective reconstruction of a known situation. Each of these approaches has its potential weaknesses and individual strengths. In the American method there is a danger of straying so far from the source in its reality that the final product loses in warmth and communicable fervor, whatever it may have gained in perception. In the German dance there are inherent the dangers of looseness of form, obscurity, and the attendant evils of mere self-expressionism. Properly controlled, however, and disciplined in its medium, this approach lends depth, radiance, and emotional conviction to the dancer's effort. Properly disciplined, I believe that the awakening and stimulation of confidence in instinct and emotion can be a valuable contribution to the education of the American dancer. The German pedagogical technique employs for this end improvisation on emotional as well as functional themes, aimed first at freedom of expression, but ultimately toward integrated composition. Without form we cannot speak of art, but the form must be an integer, not a superimposed part on the whole and must glow unmistakably with that inner flame which is its source and its significance.

This subjective and emotional approach colors even more subtly the use of space characteristic of the German dancer, accounting at least in part for the unfailing consciousness of space, actual and created, as a factor of the greatest importance. Space, rhythm, volume, and proportion are realized by both the German and the American dancer of first rank. But the use of space as an emotional element, an active partner in the dance, is distinctly European. Possibly because of a past more complex and a destiny more at the mercy of outer forces than is the case in America, we have become aware of the dramatic implications in the vision of the individual pitted against the universe. Space, with its constrictions and its immensity, its dark vistas and blinding horizons, becomes for the dancer an invitation or a menace, but in any case, an inescapable element. The American dancer seems frequently to have little use, to be but slightly aware of space except as an incidental factor in design and floor pattern. Perhaps it is because the American background has had no external obstructions to their conquest of the vastness of their continent, because distances have succumbed with relatively little struggle to the pioneer's onward march, that the American dancer stands above and so often untouched by space as an active agent.

Mary Wigman, from whose genius and early experiments the entire German dance derived its present standing, illustrates perfectly this intimate feeling for space. Those of us who worked with her at the start of her career will be forever permeated with those fundamental principles toward which she has always striven. In the realm of space particularly, I feel that Mary Wigman has made a great contribution to the contemporary dance. In her dances she alternately grapples with space as an opponent and caresses it as though it were a living, sentient thing. In her gestures and movements she carves boldly and delicately visible and fluid forms, shaping, surrounding, and sinking into the space which presses close about her.

Similarly, this emotional impetus makes its influence felt even in the physical techniques of the moving body. Superb and precise as is the technical virtuosity of even the less than great American dancers, their approach and interest are usually directed toward bodily accomplishment for its own sake. Even though a given dance may be composed to convey an emotional theme, the mechanics used in its externalization will have been separately developed. A gesture and movement vocabulary are first prepared and only subsequently employed in various combinations for various ends. This can be done with finished and brilliant results, but it is an approach radically different from that of the German dancer. For us each composition evolves through its own emotional demands, not only its special gestures, but more important still, its particular tension and even its distinctive technique.[10]

Rudolf von Laban had become in 1930 director of the Allied State Theaters of Berlin and in this capacity produced in the following years many compositions of "movement choirs." Hanya Holm's first major American composition, *Trend* (premiered in 1937 at the Bennington College Summer Dance Festival), was a

FIGURE 49. *Trend* (United States, 1937)

work of the same tradition: a great choral piece of interflowing
forms, magnificently illustrating the dynamic and expressional
force of such an architecture, subjectively inspired, unfolding as
though sculpturing space. The influence of the early Dalcroze
years, both on Holm's own art and on Wigman's, was also evident in this musical visualization, danced to a prerecorded score
for nonorchestral instruments. In 1941 she established in Colorado Springs the Center of Dance in the West, where she has
been conducting annual summer courses for no less than forty
years. And that she indeed succeeded in adapting her German
ideals of dance to the American land and temper is evident, not
only from the popularity of the Broadway musical plays that
she choreographed—*Kiss Me, Kate* (1948), *My Fair Lady* (1956),
and *Camelot* (1960)—but also from the brilliant career of her
pupil Alwin Nikolais, who was her studio assistant in the forties
and fifties. Nikolais went on to extend the application of her
principles to sound, property, and lighting effects: thus achieving a dance theater in which the entire stage, together with its
dance company, became a visualized musical score. His very

titles—*Masks, Props, and Mobiles* (1953), *Kaleidoscope* (1956), *Allegory* (1959), *Totem* (1960), and *Imago* (1963)—convey the sense of the visionary, apparitional mode and manner of his art. Each work, in its special dance technique as well as staging, illustrated the fundamental principle above enunciated by Holm; namely, that each composition should evolve out of its own demands, not only its special gestures, but also its particular tension and even distinctive technique.

CHAPTER 11

⸺⸺●⸺⸺

UNDOUBTEDLY, IT WAS THE INWARD GAZE, the explorative subjectivity of Mary Wigman's life-in-art, that brought her already in her first compositions to a breakthrough into the sphere of myth, not in the way simply of a reproduction of mythic narratives, but of felicitous aesthetic applications of the import of psychologically relevant mythic motifs: as in the use she made of a recollection of the way in which Odysseus in the Underworld summoned the shades of the dead. The psychology implicit in Laban's theory of the motivation of dance (from impulse to act) was, of course, supportive of this subjective approach, and the fact that Carl G. Jung was also at work in Zurich in her time breaking through to those zones of the Unconscious from which (as he was among the first to realize) the imagery of myth arises—these may also have had some influence on her thinking. James Joyce, likewise in Zurich, and Thomas Mann in Germany were composing their mythological novels, *Ulysses* and *The Magic Mountain*, where again we pass through the medium of art to intimations of a mythic ground reflected in life.

The philosophical tradition underlying these related movements was the same as that out of which the works of Isadora Duncan's three "European Masters" had arisen: Beethoven,

Wagner, and Nietzsche. Dating from the Middle Ages of Meister Eckhart and Wolfram von Eschenbach, its paramount modern representatives were Goethe, Hegel, and Kant. Schopenhauer recognized its profound affinities with Hindu and Buddhist thought, as did Nietzsche likewise, and Wagner. Its chief American representatives were Emerson, Thoreau, and Walt Whitman —the last of which three having been a major inspiration to Isadora: his "I Hear America Singing" became her "I See America Dancing." Briefly summarized, the fundamental thought of this finally mystical philosophy is of a primal ground beyond yet indwelling all phenomenal forms, which of living things is the life; whereas the intellect may become to such a degree overwhelmed by impressions of the outward world, arriving through the senses, that the inward voice loses force and a separation of the outward from the inward life ensues. Health, therefore, and right thinking lie in a return, through nature, to a knowledge of its metaphysical ground, which, finally, is the structuring force of all history, as well as of any properly grounded individual life. The function of both mythology and art, then, being to render to the outward mind a vision of the way to the inward life. Again, as in the words of Cézanne: "Art is a harmony parallel to nature."

In America's studios of the 1930s and early forties, on the other hand, the guiding philosophies were of Sigmund Freud and Karl Marx, the Wall Street crash of 1929 having turned all popular thought to sociology. Freud's psychology of the "Oedipus complex" (son overthrowing father) and the Marxian of revolution ("exploited" overthrowing "exploiters") nicely fused in a compound of didacticism and pornography (James Joyce's definition of "Improper Art"[1]), to which journalism, revolt, and orgasm were the Muses, offering the only tolerated subject matter and only conceivable themes. Anything else was "Ivory Tower," irrelevant, rejected, and detested. The WPA was patron. The reviewers (so-called critics) of the *New York Herald-Tribune* and the *New York Times* were the judges and executioners in the name of "All the news that fits." And against this relentless tide the cause of any studio of "proper art," or of anything like a mystic insight, was in jeopardy. "Beware," warns Nietzsche in his *Thus Spake Zarathustra*, "Beware of spitting against the wind." Or, as another has warned more strongly: "Do not give dogs what is holy; and do not cast your pearls before swine, lest they trample them underfoot and turn to attack you" (Matthew 7:6).

In the two creative New York studios (now separated from Denishawn) of Graham and Horst, Humphrey and Weidman, the emphasis aesthetically was largely on the formal or Taboo side of the art, with little of the inward, Totem.

In Doris Humphrey's theory of the dance, for instance, which she communicated to Weidman, all movement falls within what she termed the "arc between two deaths": the balanced stillness of the vertical position and inert stillness of the horizontal, on the floor—the arc between being of imbalances. Every movement out of the vertical tends to a fall beyond recovery and must be followed by a return; the more extreme and exciting the controlled fall, the more vigorous the compensatory readjustment. While every movement out of the horizontal position is of an effort. In this art, according to her thinking, there is no need, as in Isadora Duncan's or in Mary Wigman's, for an *emotional* impulse behind the dancer's movements; for by an immediate analogy with the nature of life itself—which, too, is of movements between two deaths—the rhythmic falls, recoveries, and signs of effort create a sense of meaning of themselves.

Humphrey's superb trilogy, *New Dance* (1936), demonstrated the range of expressivity that is possible to such an art of unsentimental pure movement. In *Dance of the Chosen* (1931), later and better known as *The Shakers*, she had turned for inspiration to an American folk tradition of dancing away one's sins, which brought to this particular composition a strain of religious fervor, along with its imagery of Americana. However, in the main, her art was musical and abstract, while that of Charles

Figure 50. *The Shakers* (United States, 1937)

Weidman, her partner, was of humorous pantomime and characterization. (His version of the cartoonist James Thurber's *Fables for Our Time*, composed in 1948, after Humphrey had retired from the stage, has been generally recognized as his masterpiece.) And it was only, therefore, in the later works of José Limón, formerly a leading dancer of their company, that the religious mood was brought again to this graceful art, most notably—with nobility and grandeur—in *The Moor's Pavane* (1949) and *Missa Brevis* (1958).

Only in the context of the Graham-Horst studio and association was there anything like a serious study begun of mythological themes and principles of order, and even there only after Mary Wigman's two visits to the United States in 1930 and 1931. For Martha Graham herself the period from 1923, when she left the Denishawn Company, to 1931, when she composed and danced *Primitive Mysteries* to a score by Louis Horst, had been a time of struggle and passionate search, both inwardly, for her own centers of experience, and outwardly, for the forms of an art that should be her own. In 1923 and 1924 she was a featured dancer in the *Greenwich Village Follies*, and it was then that Michio Ito introduced her to Isamu Noguchi, the sculptor who in 1935 would design the set for her signature piece, *Frontier*, again to a score by Louis Horst. In 1926, the year of her professional debut, she presented in three recitals a total of twenty-five premieres to scores by Schubert, Schumann, Debussy, Ravel, Scriabin, Satie, and many more. Strains of Denishawn are evident in such titles as *Three Gopi Maidens*, *Gypsy Portrait*, and *A Study in Lacquer*, but in at least one of the works of the next year, *Revolt*, to a score by Arthur Honegger, a sign is given of the Martha Graham to come, as well as of her intellectual engagement already in the currently incipient Marxist course. Ostensibly a dance of social protest, inwardly it was of rage against the dancer's own entanglement in the forms of an art that was not her own. Fanny Brice made fun of it in a memorable parody in the *Ziegfeld Follies* of that year, and it became the model, then, for a spate of social protest compositions that went on and on and on, through the next three decades.

The innovative personal style distinctly announced in this piece and comically imitated by Fanny Brice was severely angular in shape, aggressively percussive, dynamic in its stress on the power of the body in movement, giving such weight to it with every step to the floor that when a jump occurred it seemed a truly mighty thing of sheer victory over repression. This was a dance of heaviness and *ekstasis*, lamentation and celebration; in Graham's own view, an altogether American dance.

"An American dance," she wrote in a program note to her solo and group works of 1936, "is not a series of steps. It is infinitely more. It is a characteristic time beat, a different speed, an accent sharp and staccato. Its task is to enrich, illuminate, and intensify the American scene."[2]

Thus again, as in the other American studio (of the Humphrey-Weidman school), the initial interest of the creative artist was in the fixing of a personal style the Taboo side of the art—but in this case with the idea of a linkage of this style to the earth, the land of the artist's birth. "The task is great," Graham wrote. "It requires that the choreographer sensitize himself to his country, that he know its history, its political and geographic life, and that he direct and correlate his experiences into significant compositions of movement.... We look to the dance for affirmation, to make the spectator more keenly aware of the vigor, the humor and the variety of life. This," she concluded, "is the function of the American dance."[3]

It was almost certainly the profound emotional pull of this dedication to the geographical, historical, Totem aspect of what she thought of as her native American art that enabled Graham to pass from the negative vehemence of mere protest to the recognition of a more compelling source of positive vehemence within. A second important realization contributing to her inward turn followed in April 1930, when she was invited to dance the role of the Chosen One in Igor Stravinsky's *The Rite of Spring*, to be presented by the Philadelphia Symphony Orchestra, Leopold Stokowski conducting, with three performances in Philadelphia at the Metropolitan Opera House and two at the Metropolitan in New York. Ten months later, Graham's own *Primitive Mysteries*, to a score by Louis Horst, was premiered at the Craig Theater, along with another group work, *Bacchanale*, to a score by Wallingford Riegger, and three solos, *Rhapsodics*, *Primitive Canticles*, and *Dolorosa*. The sense of discovery is obvious: on the one hand, of an inward source and resource, affirmative of the ordeal of life, and on the other, of a heritage of archaic and primitive ritual forms, already expressive—and hence, evocative—of such sentiments of affirmation. A new sense of centered ease and accord, with no loss of force but a gain in formal assurance, now becomes evident in her art.

An important reinforcement to Graham's appreciation of

her native land had been gained when she and Horst together received in 1930–31 a Guggenheim grant to study the ceremonials of the Indian tribes of the Southwest. In 1935, her solo *Frontier* was composed to an elegant, minimal Noh-type set by Noguchi. In 1938, there followed the grandiose *American Document*: a festival choral piece of panoramic transformations, celebrating the land, folk, ideals, and democratic declarations of the republic of her own historical heritage, sumptuously presented in Carnegie Hall in a benefit performance for *The New Masses*. (These were the years of the so-called United Front.) The work was the most pretentious and last of the artist's politically didactic compositions and already contained the seeds (though as yet no visible signs) of an important shift in both the dance technique and the personal psychology of the artist.[4]

For in it she had introduced for the first time the figure of a male; namely Erick Hawkins, whom she later married. All the earlier works had been composed either for herself alone or for herself with a company of women—being even aggressively female in accent, with a heavy, violently thumping and thrusting, cruising about on the stage of well-drilled phalanxes of Amazons. Now, for the first time, she appears not as the female world-center—whether of history (as in *Frontier*) or of some cult (as in *Primitive Mysteries*), the Feminine Androgyne—but as a female in relation to a male. And the immediate consequences, not only in dance technique, but also in the matter of her concept of a dance, appeared in the triad of poetical works that immediately followed:

Every Soul Is a Circus (1939), where she danced the part of a silly woman, neurotically at bay between a master male (Erick Hawkins) and a puckish youth (Merce Cunningham, whose first New York appearance was made in this attractive role, bearing in hand upright before his face a prodigious artificial chrysanthemum);

El Penitente (1940), which was a mystery play inspired by the Good Friday rites of the *Penitentes* of New Mexico, in which

Graham danced the interfused three female roles of Temptress, Co-Savior, and Mater Dolorosa to the suffering Penitent
(Hawkins), who was judged and restored by a figure of the Sav-
ior (Cunningham); and finally, *Letter to the World* (again 1940),
the culminating masterpiece of this phase of her career.

This was a tenderly conceived and realized portrait of the soul
and world of the poet Emily Dickinson, with Jean Erdman and
Martha Graham herself in the roles, respectively, of Emily's mind
and heart, Erick Hawkins as the lost lover, Merce Cunningham as
the blithe spirit of life's springtime, and Jane Dudley (a longtime
member of the company) as "The Postponeless Creature," Death
in Time. These three dance plays were of a literary genre not seen
before on the modern dance stage: *El Penitente*, built on a mythic
theme; *Circus* and *Letter*, threaded, respectively, on spoken lines
from Vachel Lindsay and Emily Dickinson. Moreover, the types
of movement invented—not only for Graham herself in her differing roles, but also for her company—were far indeed from her
earlier, aggressively impersonal, percussive style.

FIGURE 51. *Letter to the World* featuring Martha Graham (left) and Jean
Erdman (right) (United States, 1945)

For, in the first place, Hawkins had never studied with her, but arrived from the ballet; and indeed, instead of subjecting him to her own disciplines, she sent her company to school with him. Cunningham, who had come to New York together with the composer John Cage from the Cornish School of Fine and Applied Arts in Seattle, had started as a tap dancer.[5] To train him for her own stage, Graham sent him for a season to Lincoln Kirstein's School of American Ballet.[6] While Erdman, who was from Hawaii and, like Cunningham and Hawkins, a fresh addition to the company, had studied from girlhood the Duncan dance and hula, as well as something of the Japanese *odori*. To her speaking role in *Letter to the World*, composed by Graham in counterpoint to her own heavier, striding style of spiritual protest and endurance, Erdman brought a characteristic fluidity and grace of dance and gesture quite her own.[7]

CHAPTER 12

———————————●———————————

OUR CHRONICLE OF THE ENTRANCE OF MYTHOLOGY into the shaping of the modern American dance movement at this point breaks into four distinct yet interlocking courses. At that time there was a certain affinity in the fluent styles of Cunningham and Erdman, so that, in 1942, John Cage suggested they should prepare a joint concert for which he would compose the music.[1] They opened at the Bennington Summer School that year and, six months later, performed at the Arts Club of Chicago to a devastating review in the Chicago *Daily Tribune* (February 15, 1943). Headline: "Young Dancers Give Program Empty of Merit."[2] The recital included three Erdman solos that remained for three decades in her repertoire, touring the world: *The Transformations of Medusa*, to a piano score composed for it by Louis Horst; *Creature on a Journey*, to a percussion composition by Lou Harrison; and *Forever and Sunsmell*, to E. E. Cummings's poem by that name, to which Cage had composed for the dancer a song for mezzo-soprano.[3] Cunningham's three solos—*Totem Ancestor*, *Shimmera*, and *In the Name of the Holocaust*—were all to scores by Cage, as was the first of the couple's two duets, *Credo in US* (a wry satire on the boredom of suburban life);[4] their second, *Ad Lib*, being to a score by Gregory Tucker. "Will modern dancers," wrote the reviewer, "please stop employing music altogether, or

else begin to show some respect for the fact, demonstrated peren-
nially by ballet, that music need not be devoid of content in order to serve as satisfactory dance accompaniment?...And when
dancers call their compositions *In the Name of the Holocaust* and
Forever and Sunsmell and *Credo in US*, they have taken nine
counts before the curtain goes up."

Martha Graham, meanwhile, was adding Erick Hawkins's
compositions to her programs, and on one occasion, he invited
Erdman to perform with him. But in a very deep way, the natural gift and aesthetic aims of these four creative personalities
were distinct, and in the end, the four went apart.

Graham and Hawkins remained the longest together, and
it was during the years of their collaboration that mythology
entered fundamentally into the structuring of both careers. At
the Bennington summer session of 1942, in a round of conversation with Jean Erdman and myself, Graham had grasped the
idea of the essential relevance of mythic themes and thinking,
on the one hand, to psychology and, on the other, to aesthetics—to her understanding, for example, of the psychological
depth of impact that such works as Stravinsky's *Rite of Spring*
and her own *Primitive Mysteries* had had upon her. Hawkins,
by then her husband, furthermore, had been a classical scholar
before committing himself to the dance, and Isamu Noguchi,
by whom her sets and props were now to be executed, had been
for years a student of mythic lore and oriental thought. She had
lately completed *Letter to the World*, with Erdman, Hawkins,
Cunningham, and Jane Dudley in the major roles, was at work
on *Deaths and Entrances*, and in 1945 would commence her labors on the great series of Greek dance plays that opened with
Cave of the Heart (1946) and *Errand into the Maze* (1947), and
moving on to *Clytemnestra* (1958), *Alcestis* (1960), *Phaedra* (1962),
and *Circe* (1963). The combination of psychological, mythic, and
aesthetic considerations had so fired her imagination that she had
embarked through the medium of her art, in a powerful series of
symbolic dramas, upon a mythically inspired spiritual journey

of her own. Her style having regained every bit of its earlier vehemence was now no longer female to the male, but the female
will, overcoming obstacles to its own unassisted tragic triumphs.
Reconfirmed in the formal features and principles of her art, she
was thus empowered to unfold through a consistent sequence of
transpersonally inspired creations a chronicle of her own interior
development, as mirrored through a selection of classical (and
then later, biblical) legends.

Erick Hawkins, of a much more composed Apollonian—in
contrast to Dionysian—temper, had as his aim in dance nothing so compelled from within, but an architecture of movement
in accord with the beauty of the human body at home in space
and time. His classical scholarship had long familiarized him
with principles of mythic narrative, and a lifetime interest in
the American Indian had familiarized him with the forms of
dance and music, as well as the mythic tales of native America.
After his separation from Graham in 1949,[5] he remained for five
years out of sight, until in 1954, he reappeared in a full evening
entitled *Here and Now with Watchers*, to an atmospheric percussion score by Lucia Dlugoszewski.[6]

Whereas Graham in all her attacks in movement had been
percussive and abruptly interrupted, giving the sense, thus, of
a store of strength not expended and of power not unleashed,
Hawkins—as was evident in this work—had eliminated all percussive shocks and tensions, returning to the flow of the ballet,
though not to the turned-out thighs and extreme crossed-foot
fifth position. Instead, he retained the parallel foot position of
the native American Indians in their dances, of which Graham
had learned during her years with Denishawn and then adopted
as a grounding feature in her own deliberate primitivism. The
uncorseted, released torso was of course retained as it had been
by all of the Moderns since Isadora. Nor did he strive for anything like the lighter-than-air effects so special to the ballet, for
which the rigid, perfectly centered spine directly over the re-
bounding foot is an essential. Rather, his achievement was of

an art that is neither of the air nor of the weight of rocks, but terrestrial, of the good earth and its children, animal as well as human, pristine, innocent, and uncontrived, in the mode and spirit of a mythic dawn—as, most recently, for example, in his *Plains Daybreak* (1979). Thus, in a very different way from Graham, though also through a season of intensive inward search combined with technical exploration, Hawkins discovered, not only his own mythological home, but also an art, sufficient in itself, to render visible the wonder of his findings there in the image of a timeless dream.

Figure 52. Merce Cunningham (right) and company (Iran, 1972)

Merce Cunningham, on the other hand, who likewise had been trained in both balletic and Graham dance techniques, arrived at an opposite constellation of stylistic decisions. In the feet he held on to the crossed fifth position as a base, for the flexibility that it gives, while using the parallel position as well. To the articulation of arms and legs of the ballet, he added articulation, not only of the torso, but of all parts of the body against each other. The only pulsation within that Graham had allowed had been of the torso, her "contraction and release," a bending forward and arching back of the spinal axis. Retaining this feature, Cunningham went further. Dividing the torso into two or three parts, he pulsated each of these separately, so that his technique became dexterous and difficult to learn. His musical director remained John Cage, who, during the fifties, was moving in his own development through a stage of rehabilitated Dada into which Cunningham comfortably followed. The device of creation by way of chance and accident—first explored by Marcel Duchamp in *3 Standard Stoppages* (1913–14) and Hans (Jean) Arp in *Collage with Squares Arranged According to the Laws of Chance* (1916–17)—was employed along with a number of other inventions both for Cage's musical and Cunningham's dance compositions. For example, Cage's *Imaginary Landscape No. 4* (1951), a score for twelve radios, twenty-four manipulators of the tuning pegs, and Cage himself in white tie and tails as the disregarded conductor; or three years later, *4'33"* (1952), a silent piece for any instrument or combination, which Cunningham matched with motionless dance. Cage's discovery of Daisetz T. Suzuki's *The Zen Doctrine of No-mind* and R. H. Blyth's *Zen in English Literature and Oriental Classics* had by now assisted him to a philosophical position ("All is impermanent, all is without a self!") that nicely matched not only his own already formulated musical aesthetic, but also the quick, flashing articulations of Cunningham's puckish stage presence and manner of action: his special use of Graham's percussive attacks, not so much to suggest power and strength, as to play the parts against each other in sudden transformations. Already in his earliest pieces Cunningham had appeared as a visitant from some other sphere: *Totem Ancestor* (1942), *Root of an Unfocus* (1944), and *Mysterious Adventure* (1945).[7]

Jean Erdman's development of a mythologically inspired art was based on her direct experience of oriental and other non-Western dance forms and theater. At home, in Hawaii, her studies had commenced with the hula and Duncan dance. The year before entering the Graham group she was introduced, on a world study-tour, not only to the dance and dancers of Java, Bali, and India, but also to their underlying mythologies and aesthetic philosophies.[8] After leaving Graham in 1943, she studied Spanish dance with José Fernandez; T'ai Chi Chuan with Chao-Li Chi; the chants, music, and hulas of old Hawaii with Mary Kawena Pukui; ballet with Muriel Stuart at the School of American Ballet; Japanese *odori* at the Honolulu Hisamatsu School; and with Pearl Primus, Haitian-African dance in exchange for lessons in the hula. Her first major composition, *The Transformations of Medusa* (1942)—Part 1, Temple Virgin; Part 2, Lady of the Wild Things; Part 3, Queen of Gorgons—was in three contrasting styles, inspired by Greek vase paintings, each reflecting in rhythmic organization the psychological resonance of its mythic theme. Her second, *Forever and Sunsmell* (1942), to a song composed for her by John Cage to a poem by E. E. Cummings, epitomized in its two contrasting styles (curvilinear, flowing, and light, against reaching, rushed, and interrupted) the psychological modes of the poet's two contrasted images—"He whose each foot loves the here of this earth" against "daughters of ifbut, offspring of hopefear." While in her third dance, *Creature on a Journey* (1943), the gliding movements over ground of the little girl dancers of Bali and their sharp, quick, birdlike changes of direction were the inspiration of a dance to convey the comical image of a fabulous bird preparing to go, and finally departing, on a journey of discovery. The percussion score by Lou Harrison perfectly matched the mood and style of the piece, which differed completely, in every sense—shape and movement, dynamic and rhythm—from the works to which Cage and Horst had composed the scores. "The style," Erdman has declared, "belongs to the dance, not to the dancer." And indeed, as Nietzsche observed: "One is an artist to the extent that one feels that what nonartists call the 'form' is in fact the content."[9] "In each of the differing styles," states Erdman, "of the Chinese,

Hindu, Spanish, Polynesian, and other regional traditions, the psychological stance of an entire people is epitomized.

"And within the arena of each such defined position the choreographic inventions only ring changes on a theme already announced."[10] And once again to quote Nietzsche: "Every style is a good style that effectively communicates an inward stance."[11]

CHAPTER 13

———————•———————

WITHIN WHAT WAS ORIGINALLY the Western but is now the global sphere of our demythologized, scientifically and economically grounded, industrial civilization, there has been such a history of rapid change in the past two hundred years that no generally held inward stand has become stabilized. All is in flux, and the individual artist is on his own, to achieve and render a style.

James Joyce in *A Portrait of the Artist as a Young Man* distinguishes between what he terms the "lyrical" form of art, "wherein the artist presents his image in immediate relation to himself," and the "dramatic," "wherein he presents his image in immediate relation to others."[1] Joyce himself chose the dramatic form, his style changing with the idea and object of each chapter. And in the field of the visual arts, it was Paul Klee, as already noticed, who most sensitively followed this rule, his style and even choice of media changing, often radically, with each picture. Comparably, in the American modern dance, the artist whose entire repertory is in exactly this sense dramatic is Jean Erdman.

It is the recognition in the object of a mythic association to which the inward life and imagination of the artist intuitively responds; and then, out of this recognition—this "crisis of the

FIGURE 53. Jean Erdman in *The Transformations of Medusa* (United States, 1942)

object" (to use Dalí's fortunate term)—the formal impulse springs: in a dance, for example, the body-shape and move-ment, dynamic and rhythm; in a painting, every decision as to medium, color, and rhythmic organization; in prose, the pace, verbal associations, and coloration, and so on.

The service to the artist of the mythic reference, therefore, is twofold. Firstly, it opens his eye to a range of associations beyond those of his personal experience, yet deeply known to his life (in the sense of Jung's "Collective Unconscious"), and secondly, it disengages whatever traditional forms may have been brought into the composition from their specifically ethnic orders of reference by revealing through their rhythms and shapes the archetypology of a transhistorical order of mind. In the art of Michio Ito, this depersonalizing function was served both by his musical inspiration and by the geometrical structuring of his choreographies. In the development of Erdman's art, there was added to these her understanding of the structuring capacity of myth, as well as the broad range of her knowledge of primitive and oriental, as well as occidental, mythological orders.

The years 1942 to 1945 in New York had about them an air of unreality. All the young men of the city were in Europe, fighting and dying in somebody else's war. Erdman caught the sense of it in a beautiful trio—*Daughters of the Lonesome Isle*— to a score for the "prepared piano" by John Cage. The mythic spell of the Celtic "Isle of Women" of fairytale and legend, Avalon, the Triple Goddess, and the classical Hesperides, hang over the piece like an enchantment.[2] A second trio, *Changing Moment* (also 1945), to a nervously tense and complex score by Harrison, brought the mood to the point of breaking. And the following year, it broke in a powerful solo that became, so to say, Jean Erdman's signature piece, *Ophelia* (1946), again to a score by Cage. *The Perilous Chapel* (1949), to a score by Harrison —its title referring to a theme from Arthurian legend of an event in the Forest Adventurous—was a group piece, again of Celtic enchantment, but of rapture now, which received the *Dance Magazine* award for the best new work of the season. The years following 1954, when she departed from New York on a solo tour to California, Hawaii, Japan, India, and back again to New York, represented a decade of enormous productivity, not only as an artist in residence for seven seasons at the University of Colorado[3] and head of the Dance Department at Bard College, but also as an independent choreographer with her own performing company and studio in New York, where she was creating and producing more than three major works a year.

A distinguishing characteristic of the programs of Erdman was her organization of the sequence of their dances to suggest

FIGURE 54. Jean Erdman in *Hamadryad* (United States, 1948)

the stages of an aesthetically rendered mythic or visionary journey. Her first full concert at the Hunter Playhouse, New York,
for example, commenced with a brilliant quartet: *And a Gigue*,
to Scarlatti; followed by a solo to Debussy, *Hamadryad*, which
introduced the mythic mood; then *Daughters of the Lonesome Isle*
and *Ophelia*, both to music by Cage; and *Sea Deep: A Dreamy
Drama*, to a score by Bernardo Segall, where Erdman herself
danced the bewildered dreamer, Donald McKayle her dream
man, while a triad of nymphs or watery Graces enspelled them
in nets of kelp. Following the intermission, the movement began to release and rapture: first the solo *En Pèlerinage*, to a score
by Erik Satie; then *Changing Moment*, to Harrison's score; *Passage*, a solo of birdlike flight to a score composed for it by Otto
Janowitz;[4] and finally, *The Perilous Chapel*, with a program note
from the Apocalypse: "and I saw a new heaven and a new earth;
for the first heaven and the first earth were passed away; and
there was no more sea."

Among the major works of this rich period of her career was a large group celebration, *Solstice* (1950), to an orchestral score by Lou Harrison, wherein for the first time she composed to a set of beautiful masks by Carlus Dyer: Donald McKayle danced the Moon-Bull and Merce Cunningham the Sun-Lion, and herself the role of the Bride of Spring to a surging chorus of animal nymphs.[5] Two spellbound solos, *Upon Enchanted Ground* (1951) and *Dawn Song* (1952), to scores composed for them by Alan Hovhaness, were followed by (among many others) an austere group work, *Broken City* (1953), to a Schoenberg score, and a major three-part solo, *Changing Woman* (1954), to which Henry Cowell composed a stunning percussion accompaniment: Part 1, Forest Voice (Wind Voice / Brook Voice / Earth Voice); Part 2, Sea Voice / Desert Voice; and Part 3, Moon Voice. Another important creation of this period was a masked solo to a score by Bartok, *Pierrot, the Moon* (1954), combining dance and mime, with its mask as well as moon and lute designed for her by Yuji Ito.

FIGURE 55. Jean Erdman with a prop from *Pierrot, the Moon* (India, 1955)

The representative solos that she carried on her triumphant world tour of 1954–55 (the first solo tour, ever, of an American dancer in the Orient) comprised *Salutatio, Ophelia, Creature on a Journey, The Transformations of Medusa, Changing Woman, Pierrot, the Moon,* and *Bagatelle*—the shimmering closing *Bagatelle* to a score by Scarlatti. It was something, in the heat of India (in Ahmedabad, Baroda, Bombay, New Delhi, and Madras), to present a two-hour solo program of this kind, but the reward was a marvelously reassuring confirmation of the artist's guiding belief that if one composed out of the archetypes of mythology and the unconscious, it would be possible to communicate immediately across the boundaries of the cultures, on a level of fundamentally human, inward knowledge. Dance in the Orient is a major art, and the dancer (as Erdman found) an honored and respected personality. The audiences are skilled in seeing, furthermore, and the reactions everywhere were of enthusiastic appreciation. The auditorium in New Delhi, where Indira Gandhi was the guest of honor, was packed to the doors, and the disgruntled Russian embassy staff sought to cover and outdo the concert by advertising for the same hour a TV broadcast of some works of the Bolshoi Ballet. Indeed, even the American embassy took notice. For Erdman's tour had been sponsored, not from Washington, but by invitations from Japanese and Indian connoisseurs and theater units. At the Academy of Music in Madras, the foremost dancer of India, Balasaraswati, presented for Erdman alone, as a gesture of gracious thanks for the dances she had brought to India, a performance of six dances in the *Bharatanatyam* style, while Professor Bhagavan, of the University of Madras, interpreted and explained the mudras and themes. *Creature on a Journey,* in particular, had been greeted throughout as a dance in the Indian spirit.[6]

The return to New York marked the beginning of a new and even richer, more expansive era in the development of a mythologically inspired dance and stage tradition by Erdman. For the next five years, at the height of her powers, she toured the United States, solo, adding to her program *Four Portraits from Duke Ellington's Shakespeare Album* (1958), and five elegant solos to music by Ezra Laderman: *Duet for Flute and Dancer* (1956), a virtuosic piece danced to rhythms established by the composer to balance and counterpoint the brilliant challenges of a flute;[7] *Fearful Symmetry* (1957), inspired by William Blake's poem "The Tyger," where the dancer appears within a large sculptural construction, by Carlus Dyer, of aluminum, out of which she emerges to dance to it, then in dialogue; and *The Road of No Return, Now and Zen—Remembering,* and *Solos and Chorale* (all 1959), the last with all the musicians on stage and the dancer circling among them.

The visit to the Orient and her experiences there of Kabuki and Noh, *Bharatanatyam* and Kathakali, had refreshed in Erdman's mind an intention that she had long been cherishing, namely, of creating works which, like those of the oriental stage, should unite the arts of music, dance, acting, mime, and stage design. In *Pierrot, the Moon,* she had moved in that direction. The masks and props for that piece had been created for her by Yuji Ito, Michio Ito's brother, whose beautiful wife, Teiko, was a member of the dance community of New York, performing in various oriental styles on the concert stages. Teiji Ito, their son, had been born to the oriental stage, so to speak; had since childhood accompanied his mother's dances and was an accomplished percussionist, as well as a performer on both string instruments and wind. When Erdman thought, therefore, of a composer to collaborate in her first serious venture toward Total Theater, a long group work for seven dancers and an actor, *Twenty Poems of e. e. cummings* (1960), it was to Teiji Ito she turned.

During the hours, meanwhile, of air travel in the course of her solo tours, she had been reading and re-reading James Joyce's *Finnegans Wake,* speculating on the possibility of a dance dedicated to the mythic heroine of that mercurial work—"ever the same, yet changing ever"—Anna Livia Plurabelle.[8] Something of the kind she had already represented in her dance *Changing*

Woman, inspired by a Navaho mythic theme, to which Henry
Cowell had composed the accompaniment. The new work,
however, would be larger; and as she pondered on it, the format
grew. In the end she assembled four actors: Anita Dangler and
Sheila Roy for the elder and younger female roles; Leonard Frey
and Van Dexter as the elder and younger males; and with herself
in the dancing parts. Teiji Ito composed the score (for an orchestra of fourteen instruments, played by three musicians), and
The Coach with the Six Insides came into being. It opened in the
fall of 1962 in the Village South Theater in Greenwich Village.
In the summer of 1963, in Spoleto, Italy, at the Festival of Two
Worlds, the Italians compared it to their commedia dell'arte;
in Paris at the Théâtre des Nations, it was compared by French
to their mime; at the Dublin Theater Festival, that fall, it was
greeted by the Irish as a work of their own; and in Tokyo, in
the spring of 1964 (following a tour of the United States), it was

Figure 56. *The Coach with the Six Insides* (United States, 1964)

recognized as a form of modern Kabuki. In New York it received the Drama Desk Award for Outstanding Achievement in the Off-Broadway Theater, the *Village Voice* Obie (Off-Broadway) Award, and in 1967, following a history of three years touring the United States, it appeared at the East 74th Street Theater for its second New York run.

In the meantime Erdman had become Founding Director of the Dance Program at the New York University School of the Arts, and in collaboration with Michael Czajkowski, a member of the music faculty, composed a series of large-scale group works to his electronic music scores; among them, *Love, Song, Dance* (1968), *Safari* (1968), and *Vulnerable as an Island Is Paradise* (1969). Another large group work, *The Castle*, composed and produced in dialogue with the virtuoso saxophonist Jimmy Giuffre, as an elaborate symbolic display of magical appearances, transformations, and disappearances, was first performed at New York University; then with a second company at the University of California in Los Angeles (1967), where Erdman was, for the first time, artist in residence; and finally with still another company and setting at the Brooklyn Academy of Music (1970). Completing the exercises of these five extraordinarily active years were two group works to scores by Laderman, *Encounter in the Grove* (1967) and *Twilight Wind* (1970); a full-evening cluster of comic compositions for a summer festival at the East-West Center in Honolulu (1969); and the choreographic structuring of three plays—Jean Cocteau's *The Wedding on the Eiffel Tower* (1967), for the Atlantic Municipal Theater; a dramatization of Israel Zangwill's *The King of Schnorrers* (1969), at the Goodspeed Opera House, East Haddam, Connecticut; and Joseph Papp's musical production to a score by Galt MacDermot, first in Central Park, then on Broadway, of Shakespeare's *The Two Gentlemen of Verona* (1970). This period culminated in the founding of her own Theater of the Open Eye and return to the endeavor, which had begun with *The Coach with the Six Insides*, of developing a mythologically grounded art of Total Theater. For *The Two Gentlemen of Verona* she had received both a Tony nomination and the Drama Desk Award for Choreography.

The first Total Theater productions at the Open Eye were a series of Yeats's *Plays for Dancers: The Herne's Egg, Calvary, A Full Moon in March*, and *The Cat and the Moon* (1972), followed by *The Only Jealousy of Emer* (1973). The approach here was not as it had been for Yeats in his presentation of *At the Hawk's Well* with Michio Ito as the only dancer, that of a poet conceiving a dramatic form of such simplicity that it might be played, as he expressed his aim, "in our sitting room...having no need of mob or press to pay its way," and so that "its few properties can be packed up in a box or hung upon the walls where they will be fine ornaments."[9] The dancer and the choreographer, with all the means of the modern stage at hand, were concerned, rather, to amplify and render visible, as well as audible, the poetry of the plays, using rhythms and dynamics, shapes and movements, lighting, color, costumes and masks, in accord. Her craft, through the years, had evolved to cope with more and more materials, responding from the beginning to suggestions emanating from structures musically, mythologically, or poetically grounded, and translating these into dances not bound to any prestated form, but, so to say, uncorseted—in Joyce's sense, "dramatic": in immediate relation to the conceived idea and not to some ethnic or personal manner of style. In her earliest works the idea came first, then the dance, and then music composed to the dance—by Horst, Cage, Harrison, Hovhaness, Janowitz, or Cowell. Later on, she began accepting her ideas of form and forming from works already composed—by Debussy, Satie, Scarlatti, Poulenc, Mozart, Prokofiev, or Schoenberg. During the years of her collaboration with Laderman, she yielded even further to dictation from the musical score, in their *Duet for Flute and Dancer*, for instance, moving beat for beat to his fixed notations. Her next step was to render in body, shape, and movement, in rhythm and dynamics, visual images equivalent to those rendered verbally in recited poetry, as in her *Twenty Poems of e. e. cummings*. And it was here that the art of Teiji Ito came best to her support, since he worked as a practicing musician, on the dance floor itself, participating in the rhythms and dynamics of the visualizations with an understanding of the space needed for words and dance. With *Finnegans Wake (The Coach with the Six Insides)*, actors and mime were added to the composition, slide-projected stage settings, narrative scenes, dream sequences, and metamorphoses with mythological overtones. A new art was born—not easily imitated. As one of the reviewers remarked when in 1979 the play was revived at the Open Eye: "*The Coach with the Six Insides* was an avant-garde event fifteen years ago, and it still is."[10]

Erdman's stagings of the *Plays for Dancers* of the Irish poet Yeats were not imitative of the Japanese Noh, though composed from the same list of elements: music, dance, poetic speech and song, symbolic sets, and masks. Other means than those of the highly stylized, sixteenth-century oriental theater were used for slowing and arresting action, extending dramatic moments, rendering a magical spell, and suggesting timeless silences beyond and within the words and acts. A knowledge, not only of the Irish legends underlying Yeats's imagery, but also of the archetypal mythological background out of which those legends originally sprang, opened ranges of associated myths and tales to her mind, from which suggestions for extensions of the references of Yeats's locally Irish subject matter could be drawn. For his poetry was thoroughly grounded in myth. Its images resonated in expanding circles of mythological associations that could be picked up visually in shapes and movements, and then rhythmically composed to accord with both the pace and the sense of his lines. Erdman's stagings were thus of a kind of archaic drama (unknown to modern actors and directors), which is visual, presentational, not verbal and discursive. In such a work the entire stage participates through choreographed transformations, in the way of a universal dance. The shapes and movements seen, and the music heard, evoke archetypal, mythological memories, awakened as it were, by the magic of the poet's lines from a night into which they return—to remain. There is a Chinese saying of the character of such a work of art: "The sound stops; the sense flows on."

Two more mythopoetic creations in the manner of this (in Joyce's sense) "dramatic" dance technique brought to culmination the years of work by Jean Erdman in Total Theater. *Gauguin in Tahiti* (1976), the first, brought into contrast and conflict the imagery, arts, ideals, and loyalties of the two orders of the mind, as reflected in the life, the works, and the spiritual as well as social and physical agony of a major European artist. Two casts—a Polynesian company of dancers, actors, and musicians from Tahiti, Hawaii, and Samoa, and the New York company of the Open Eye, with Kevin O'Connor as Gauguin—performed throughout in counterpoint as images of the man's tortured yet, in its art, triumphant mind. Projections of his paintings in a sequence of increasing wonder filled the stage in grim moments of his breaking body and heart's greatest anguish, while a recurrent choral dancing and chanting of traditional ceremonial passages by the Polynesian company provided a mythic foil—like that of the classical Greek chorus—against which the ordeal of the truly extraordinary biography acquired the character of a spiritual self-immolation.

The second creation, *The Shining House* (1979–80) shifts the action from the human to the mythological plane with an old Hawaiian legend of the dangerous volcano goddess Pele and her betrayed but loyal sister, Hi'iaka. In a colorful, ever-changing environment produced by the projected abstract paintings of Paul Jenkins, and to an electronic score by Michael Czajkowski, an atmosphere of fairytale is rendered for a masque in dance and song of two divine sisters contending for a youthful king. It is an age-old story, in its own way, of Aphrodite and the goddess of the underworld, Persephone, contending for Adonis. Masks have returned (there were no masks in *Gauguin*): flame-like, flower-like. That of Pele is of the hideous hag, but then again, the seductress. And this, too, is a familiar motif from the fairy-tales of all the world.

The universality of many of the images, themes, and even story patterns of mythology has long been recognized as a reality to be explained, and one obvious explanation has been that the shared plots, themes, and images must have been spread about the world by diffusion. For instance, in relation to Erdman's legend of Pele and Hi'iaka, it appears that in old Hawaii there was a pig-god, Kamapua'a, who was associated with Pele as her ravisher and lover. Pig sacrifices, furthermore, were associated with her rites. But in ancient Greece, as well, in the rites addressed to Persephone in the underworld, pig sacrifices were customary. Moreover, there was a divine swineherd or pig-god named Eubuleus, who seems to have been present, together with his herd, just when Persephone was ravished to the underworld by Hades; and according to Sir James Frazer, in *The Golden Bough*,[11] this pig-god was a mythological doublet of the ravisher, Hades, himself. Still further, in Ireland, where the Hideous Hag / Beautiful Seductress theme is a prominent one in both mythology and folklore, there is the legend of a great lover, Diarmuid, who was slain, like the Greek Adonis, by a boar.

Yeats, in *A Full Moon in March*, brings onto his stage an Irish swineherd, to be sacrificed by a virgin queen, whose severed head then sings to her of the mystery beyond death. Yeats knew, of course, that the March full moon is the moon of Good Friday and Easter; also, that the moon (the celestial severed head), ever waning and waxing, is the heavenly sign in many mythologies of a life to be gained beyond death. In certain islands of the Pacific, where the crescent tusks of sacrificed boars are likened to the two crescents of the waning and waxing moon, the severed heads of the offered animals are preserved on racks as signs to their owners of a promise of eternal life.[12]

Yeat's *Irish* play for dancers and Jean Erdman's *Hawaiian* are thus based, respectively, on legends from the two extremes of what was once, apparently, a single prehistoric province of swine domestication. And it can be suggested, consequently, that with the early diffusion (from circa 10,000 B.C. or so) of the custom of domesticating pigs, there must have traveled, also, a ritual of pig sacrifice and, along with that, the mythology of a pig-god and his goddess to whom the sacrifices were addressed.

The alternative explanation (by many scholars preferred) comes to this problem of the distribution of myths from a psychological viewpoint, observing that since the human mind, like the body, is everywhere essentially the same, responding in like ways to a human lifetime's fundamental experiences, it is inevitable that similar myths should have arisen, practically everywhere, independently of historical contact. Everywhere, for example, throughout the spectacle of nature, beyond the changing shape of things, there are patterns, types, or presences to be recognized, which are enduring: "ever the same," as Joyce remarks in *Finnegans Wake*, "yet changing ever." And throughout the course of a lifetime there is equally the sense of an entity enduring through all the apparent transformations, from infancy to age. A people likewise endure through all the changes of its members, who in their roles are continuing manners of thought and action established from ancestral times.

It is the function of mythology and ritual everywhere to fix the individual in the knowledge and maintenance of these enduring, universally recognized archetypes: the roles appropriate to one's age, sex, and social station; acts appropriate to the seasons of the year and of life; the mental attitudes proper to warfare and to peace, when killing and butchering beasts for food, or when disposing of the dead. As we read in a key passage of Ovid's *Metamorphoses*: "All things are changing; nothing dies. The spirit wanders, comes now here, now there, and occupies whatever frame it pleases. From beasts it passes to human bodies, and from our bodies into beasts, but never perishes. And as the pliant wax is stamped with new designs, does not remain as it was before nor keep the same form long, but is still the selfsame wax, so do I teach that the soul is ever the same, though it passes into ever-changing bodies."[13]

Or in the Hindu Bhagavad Gītā: "even as a person casts off worn-out clothes and puts on others that are new, so the embodied Self casts off worn-out bodies and enters into others that are new. Weapons cut It not; fire burns It not; water wets It not; the wind does not wither It."[14]

And with a radical change of mood, phraseology, and pathos, in Joyce's *Finnegans Wake*: "His everpresent toes are always in retaliessian out throuth his overpast boots. Hear him squak!"[15] The idea is already announced in the Egyptian Book of the Dead (third and second millennia B.C.), where the soul of the one who had died is identified with Eternity and in the chapter entitled, "On Coming Forth by Day in the Underworld," exclaims in rapture in the fullness of this knowledge: "I am Yesterday, Today and Tomorrow, and have the power to be reborn a second time. I am the divine hidden Soul who createth the gods....He is I, and I am he."[16] It is the whole sense of the Indian Upaniṣads that one should come to this rapture and knowledge while yet alive. "Knowing the great, all-pervading Self, which is bodiless among bodies, stable amidst the unstable, the steadfast one does not grieve....Though hidden in all things, this Self does not shine forth, yet is seen by those of subtle sight through one pointed, subtle intuition."[17]

But this subtle shift of vision from the outward, changing shapes of things to the informing mystery of their being—the *mysterium tremendum et fascinans* of all existing forms whatsoever—is the function, not only of mythologically grounded ritual and mystical philosophy, but also of all serious art. As phrased by the poet Gerhart Hauptmann: *Dichten heisst, hinter Wörtern das Urwort erklingen lassen*—"Poetic creativity consists in letting the Word resound behind words." And indeed, the earliest works of human art of which we have knowledge were brought forth in the service of rituals and their myths. Dance, song, rhythm, and rapture are the elements of all such performances.

Costumes and masks open the ways to vision, their inspiration being of the imagination, the inward life, not the outward, of the mind. And the festival or ceremonial in which they appear is thus an expression of the enduring, inward aspect of experience. Nietzsche, in *The Birth of Tragedy*, points to the contrast and relationship, in the classical Greek theater, of the chorus and the actors. The origins of that theater were in rituals and myth; and in the dancing, chanting chorus the mythic mode is continued. Its members are no longer individuals, but move and chant as one, representing the mystery and force of that undifferentiated primal ground out of which all forms arise and back to which they return. The actors, on the other hand, are as individuals, representative of the forms that appear in the field of space and time only to break and dissolve. The god Apollo, as the lord of the light world and the poetry of its images—whether of waking-consciousness or of dreams—is the protector and patron of the roles of the actors. Whereas it is the voice of Dionysos that is heard through the choral chants. The Greek theaters were established in the precincts of Dionysos's shrines. As the lord of rapture in the realization of one's identity with that everlasting primordial One, out of which all individuated lives briefly appear, he stands for the mythic dimension, while Apollo stands for the formal of the tragic art. Nietzsche held that these two together constituted the essential terms of all art and that in the Greek tragedy they were represented in the two features of the chorus and the actors.

In our own modern theater, however, it is evident that the arts, respectively, of the chorus and the action have been separated and separately developed: the chorus, in the dance, and the action in our drama, which, from the middle of the nineteenth century moved deliberately toward a naturalism altogether removed from the province of the original patron of both the tragic and the comic arts, Dionysos. In the novel and in the arts of painting and sculpture as well, naturalism was the prevailing aim. Only in the opera did anything else appear, and here, only with Wagner (following his encounter with Schopenhauer's orientalized philosophy) did anything like a mythologically inspired rapture come back onto our stage. Whereas in the Orient the theater never broke loose from its mythic ground, and in Japan, where historical and even contemporary characters might be introduced as protagonists, the relation of their actions to the archetypes of a mythic tradition could be always held before the mind—again as in the classical Greek theater—by the contrasting element of a chorus. As in the oriental music, the melody floats above a drone, which establishes and maintains its ground (or as in meditation the syllable OM is sounded to alert and hold the mind to the Dionysian ground of its own consciousness, and of all being and bliss whatsoever).[18] So in the Noh, as in the classical theater of the Greeks, the chorus establishes and maintains the orientation to myth, while the action unrolls to its own logic. And it was the rediscovery and recognition of the value of this archaic theatrical device that so inspired Yeats in his work with Michio Ito on *At the Hawk's Well*.

There are many ways in which the instrument can be manipulated. At the Dublin International Theater Festival, September–October 1978, and again at Jean Erdman's the Open Eye in New York, May 1980, Ulick O'Connor's *Three Noh Plays* were presented—*The Grand Inquisitor, Submarine,* and *Deirdre* —in all of which he followed exactly the Japanese pattern of, first, an entrance and seating of musicians, upstage; next, an entrance and seating of the chorus, stage left; and then, from stage right, the formal, stylized entrances, in order, of the cast. Yeats, on the other hand, who had never seen a Japanese play, invented for each of his *Plays for Dancers* an appropriate, particular scenario of introductions and interrelations of the complementary musical and narrative modes. With his ideal in mind of an unpretentious theater for the European drawing room, his usual way was to let his two or three musicians unfold a long black cloth to provide a set, while reciting a tangential poetic narrative as foil for the proposed action, and with interludes, then, of music, song, and occasionally dance, returning his musicians to the foreground in counterplay with the action. Martha Graham's way, in contrast, of bringing mythic elements into play on her stage—though largely Japanese inspired—was of a radically different aesthetic. She, too, had in her background the example of Michio Ito. In her Denishawn years, one of her principal roles had been to perform the company's Japanese dances. She was thus familiar with Japanese theater. And Isamu Noguchi, the great Japanese-American sculptor, became, for her mythologically inspired works, the designer of her sets and props. Her approach, however, was from the standpoint, not of literature, but of dance—not of Apollo, that is to say, but of Dionysos. She was not discovering a way to bring music and the dance to the support of a dramatic art, but on the contrary, had found a way to convert dance itself into a drama. There was to be no counterplay of musical and dramatic features in her art. Her narratives were of classical plays that could be assumed to be already known to her audience and were briefly summarized for them in program notes: the performance then being of sheer dance against that implied but invisible foil.

Jean Erdman's various ways of composing the two elements in her seven, greatly differing Total Theater productions illustrate the range of possibilities of such a theater, in which the two are *equally* contained. Yeats's concept had been literary: his ideal of an intimate drawing-room presentation left unregarded the possibilities of the larger proscenium stage; while Graham, from the point of view of a dancer, had assigned all literary matter to the program and on her stage presented simply—but greatly—a dance. Erdman, then, in contrast, approached her first production of the kind as a dancer and choreographer fascinated by the language of James Joyce's *Finnegans Wake*. Her desire was to render in the form of a dance the role of Anna Livia Plurabelle, but within the frame of a play that should give equal place to the miracle of Joyce's prose and the organization of his plot. The result was *The Coach with the Six Insides*, a Total Theater piece in three acts, for one dancer, four actors, and three musicians. Her next four productions were adaptations (to the proscenium stage) of Yeats's *A Full Moon in March*, *The Cat and the Moon*, *Calvary* and *The Only Jealousy of Emer*. One of the difficulties to be overcome today before work on such pieces can be undertaken is that of discovering actors who can move and dancers who can speak. The trainings are now so specialized and separate that the actor and the dancer are practically two species.[19] Erdman, fortunately, at the Open Eye, had for some seven seasons a company of performers of more than one commitment each, and with these cocreators, supported by Teiji Ito's musicians and the poetic masks of Ralph Lee, she was able to fuse formal dance and narrative dramatic action freely and throughout, in ways appropriate to each of the several plays, yet as productions of a single unified art.

The sheerly dramatic potentialities of a modern theater in which the classic arts of individual action and choral song—Apollo and Dionysos—can be brought together and fused appeared in Erdman's next masterwork, her *Gauguin in Tahiti*, where in fact, the two musical and choral arts of Europe and Polynesia were played against each other, as the two worlds of Gauguin's birth and art played in the consciousness of this at once tortured and triumphant visionary. The ritual chants and ceremonies of Tahiti and the Marquesas sounded and continued as the drone, or OM, over which the history and agony of a modern life in this modern world could be rendered in the naturalistic manner of a modern play. In her following Total Theater work, then, the accent was reversed: for whereas in Gauguin the narrative had been of the tragedy of an actual life played out against a background of mythologically inspired Polynesian ceremonials, in *The Shining House* the Polynesian mythological narrative is brought to focus, lightly and playfully, on the love games of a cluster of young people on a modern Hawaiian beach—a playful spectacle, chiefly of song and dance, in complete contrast to the earlier piece.

The range of possibilities of this type of theater is thus indeed considerable. Its reintroduction into drama of the classical principle of the chorus—a rhythmed order of speech and gesture through which the Word or Words of the Silence beyond the immediate words of the narrative are suggested—opens to the mind a dimension beyond change, which it has been everywhere the function of true poetry to make known. Under the banner of our nineteenth- (and post-nineteenth-) century requirements for naturalism, social didactic, and interesting character portrayal, however, knowledge of the classic means to this poetic type of theater had disappeared until Yeats recovered it from Japan. In the other visual arts the breakthrough can be said to have been achieved already in 1907 with Picasso's *Demoiselles d'Avignon*, where his incongruous inclusion of an African feature in the composition opened the mind to unsuspected realms of aesthetic possibilities into which the art then moved. His earlier manipulations of forms had taken off from features of the world of sight. From this moment on, his art was of apparitions—as was equally that of Paul Klee. But in our theater—especially in England and the United States—the old nineteenth century hangs on. The larger, after-dinner public is apparently in no need of anything more. Yeats recognized this fact when he turned to the idea of a modest theater apart, "having no need of mob or Press to pay its way—an aristocratic form."[20] And indeed all creative art today—as compared with popular entertainment—is necessarily of this kind. Judgments based on commercial, numerical standards, best-seller lists, and the like, cannot but view such works as peripheral, whereas, in fact, in the perspective of the history of any art, they are central and what counts. In the history of painting, this is obvious. In the history, however, of such an ephemeral form as the dance, not so! When the popular musical hit *Oklahoma* opened in 1943 to a vast Broadway acclaim, only those in the audience who for years had been watching Martha Graham, Hanya Holm, Doris

Humphrey, and Charles Weidman perform for single nights in high-school and college auditoriums would have been familiar already with every one of the dance movements that here, at one stroke, transformed the New York concept of a musical show. The day of the high-kicking chorus line was ended. Nor would anyone watching earlier Graham and the rest, who had not seen Michio Ito perform, have recognized the combination of oriental and eurythmic inspirations that underlay much of what they saw. Oswald Spengler, writing not only of the dance, but also of the act of any artist in following and exploring the rhythmic swing and flow of the living "Thou" of his inspiration, remarks that this moment of performance, or "imitation," being life, is past in the very moment of accomplishment. "The curtain falls, and it passes either into oblivion or, if the product is a durable surface, into art-history."

"Of the songs and dances of Old cultures," he continues, "nothing remains, of their pictures and poems little. And even this little contains substantially, only the ornamental [i.e. achieved, enduring, formal] side of the original imitation and the sound; of a poem only the words, not the recital; and of all their music the notes at most, not the tone-colors of the instruments. The essential is irrevocably gone, and every 'reproduction' is in reality something new and different."[21]

The opposite order of art, to this "imitation" is, in Spengler's terms, the "ornamental," as represented most clearly in architecture—the temple, the pyramid, the cathedral, which are fixed in space and endure. "An imitation," as Spengler states, "is beautiful [or ugly], an ornament significant, and therein lies the difference between direction and extension, organic logic and inorganic, life and death....Imitation spiritualizes and quickens. The one becomes, the other is. And therefore the one is allied to love, and above all—in songs and riot and dance—to the *sexual love* that turns existence to face the future; and the other to care of the past, to recollection and to the *funerary*. The beautiful is longingly pursued, the significant instills dread, and there is no deeper contrast than that between the house of the living and the house of the dead."[22]

In our modern visual and theatrical arts, however, the two have been deliberately joined. Following the moment of Picasso's *Demoiselles d'Avignon*, he proceeded, in collaboration with Georges Braque, to the development of the *ornamental* vogue of Cubism, where the forms of life were not imitated, but analyzed and reordered to an architectural composition. The imitative, naively inspired, spontaneously free dance of Isadora was succeeded by the choreographic architectures, first of Michio Ito and then of a constellation of schools. To the moment of beautiful, Apollonian joy in the rhythmic grace of a passing movement of life, the counter-rhythm is brought of the Sacrifice, the alter of Dionysos and its hieratic, *ornamental* chorus, stylized in both chant and movement according to fixed and enduring forms. Thus to beauty there is brought significance (in the sense of Spengler's use of the term), to an expression of life, the statement of a worldview. And yet, since every theatrical performance whatsoever is ephemeral, and each dancer's dancing is of him or her alone, the history of the creative moments of these arts is comparable to a marking of the passing flight of a bird in the sky or the track of a fish in the sea. One must have been there at the moment of the passing life and witnessed with a following eye that gesture of grace of the wonder informing all things.

NOTES

Editor's comments are enclosed in brackets.

EDITOR'S FOREWORD

1. Stephen and Robin Larsen, *A Fire in the Mind: The Life of Joseph Campbell* (New York: Doubleday, 1991), 250.
2. Joseph Campbell, "Symbolism and the Dance, Part 3," *Dance Observer* 17, no. 4 (April 1950), 53.
3. Larsen, *Fire in the Mind,* 255.
4. Joseph Campbell, "Betwixt the Cup and the Lip," *Dance Observer* 11, no. 3 (March 1944), 30.
5. Joseph Campbell, *The Inner Reaches of Outer Space: Metaphor as Myth and as Religion* (New York: Harper & Row, 1986), 122–32.
6. Larsen, *Fire in the Mind,* 3.
7. Ibid., 12.
8. Charles Moritz, ed., *Current Biography* 32, no. 8 (September 1971): 14–17.
9. Larsen, *Fire in the Mind,* 240.
10. Ibid., 241.
11. Ibid., 242.
12. Ibid., 243, 246.
13. Ibid., 248.
14. Ibid., 265.
15. *Dance and Myth: The World of Jean Erdman, Part 1: The Early Dances,* choreographer and artistic director Jean Erdman, producers Celia Ipiotis and Jeff Bush, director and editor Celia Ipiotis, executive producer

Nancy Allison (New York: Foundation for the Open Eye, 1990), video-cassette.

16. *Dance and Myth: The World of Jean Erdman, Part 2: The Group Dances,* choreographer and artistic director Jean Erdman, directors Nancy Allison and Dan Berkowitz, producer Dan Berkowitz, executive producer Nancy Allison (New York: Foundation for the Open Eye, 1991), videocassette.

17. Ibid.

18. Larsen, *Fire in the Mind,* 365–422.

PART I: ARTICLES AND LECTURES (1944–1978)
BETWIXT THE CUP AND THE LIP (1944)

1. [This article first appeared in the *Dance Observer* 11, no. 3 (March 1944). The *Dance Observer* was founded in 1934 by the composer and influential dance composition teacher Louis Horst as a literary forum for the choreographers, theorists, and critics of the burgeoning American modern dance movement. He served as chief critic and editor until his death in 1964.]

2. James Joyce, *Finnegans Wake* (New York: Viking Press, 1939), 412.

TEXT, OR IDEA? (1944)

1. [This article first appeared in the *Dance Observer* 11, no. 6 (June–July 1944).]

2. [George W. Beiswanger (1902–93) was a noted art critic and philosophy professor who wrote frequently for the *Dance Observer,* among other publications. He was known for his embrace of new choreographic directions, especially those of Merce Cunningham and Alwin Nikolais, and for his ability to describe them in relation to similar trends in painting, music, and theater.]

THE JUBILEE OF CONTENT AND FORM (1945)

1. [This article first appeared in the *Dance Observer* 12, no. 5 (May 1945).]

THE ANCIENT HAWAIIAN HULA (1946)

1. [This article first appeared in the *Dance Observer* 13, no. 3 (March 1946). It is an abridgement of Campbell's introductory remarks prior to a lecture demonstration of the Hawaiian hula, presented by students of Jean Erdman at the New Dance Group Lecture Series, November 11, 1945.

The New Dance Group, founded in 1932 in New York City, was

originally formed as a radical leftist political movement under the name Workers Dance League. By the time Erdman joined the group in 1943, its focus, while still political, had shifted away from labor issues and was more concerned with offering classes and performances of modern dance that were available to all races and income levels. The group served as an important artistic cauldron for the dancers and choreographers of the post-pioneering period of American modern dance, offering its member artists the opportunity to develop their approach to technique through teaching and to present their choreography in shared concerts, sometimes in a Broadway theater. In addition to teaching Hawaiian hula and fundamentals of movement (beginning level modern dance technique) at the New Dance Group School, Erdman premiered many of her early dance works in their concerts. She left the group in 1949, citing aesthetic differences. Many of the performances Campbell wrote about in chapters 1 to 3 were more than likely New Dance Group concerts.

The group was the subject of a major retrospective concert in New York City produced by the American Dance Guild in 1993. In addition, comprehensive exhibits appeared at the National Museum of Dance in Saratoga Springs, New York, in 2005–7 and at the Centre National de la Danse in Pantin, France, in 2007, which continues to tour. In 2000, the New Dance Group was honored by the Library of Congress and the Dance Heritage Coalition as one of "America's Irreplaceable Dance Treasures: The First 100," and in 2006, it was inducted into the National Dance Museum's Hall of Fame.

For more information see: *The New Dance Group Gala Concert*, director Johannes Holub, produced by Dancetime Publications in agreement with the American Dance Guild (1994), DVD.]

Symbolism and the Dance, Part 1 (1950)

1. [This article first appeared in the *Dance Observer* 17, no. 2 (February 1950). It is the first of a three-part article.]
2. In this paper I am not discussing emblems, which are visible conventional signs denoting certain objects or abstract ideas; for example, the flag as an emblem of the nation, the dove as an emblem of peace, people with tools in their hands as an emblem of the proletariat revolution, or the cross as an emblem of Christian civilization.
3. *Finnegans Wake*, 255; Genesis, 2:21–22.
4. This whole constellation of symbols has been discussed at length in my recent work *The Hero with a Thousand Faces* (Novato, CA: New World Library, 2008).

SYMBOLISM AND THE DANCE, PART 2 (1950)

1. [This article first appeared in the *Dance Observer* 17, no. 3 (March 1950). It is the second of a three-part article.]
2. A. R. Radcliffe-Brown, *The Andaman Islanders*, 2nd ed. (Cambridge: Cambridge University Press, 1933), 129–30.
3. Franz Boas, *The Mind of Primitive Man*, 1st ed. (New York: MacMillan, 1931), 87–88.
4. W. Köhler, *The Mentality of Apes* (1925), 326–27.
5. The italics are Dr. Köhler's.
6. This also was discussed in part 1 of the present paper.

SYMBOLISM AND THE DANCE, PART 3 (1950)

1. [This article first appeared in the *Dance Observer* 17, no. 4 (April 1950). It is the third of a three-part article.]
2. [For Campbell's more in-depth discussion of "the idea of a Golden Age, when man and beast had not yet differentiated," see Joseph Campbell, *Historical Atlas of World Mythology, Volume I: The Way of the Animal Powers, Part 1: Mythologies of the Primitive Hunters and Gatherers* (New York: Perennial Library, Harper & Row, 1988), 73–79, and Joseph Campbell, *The Masks of God: Primitive Mythology* (New York: Viking Press, 1959), 282–95.]
3. Alice C. Fletcher, *The Hako: A Pawnee Ceremony*, 22nd annual report, part 2 (Washington: Bureau of American Ethnology, 1904), 243–44.
4. *The Dialogues of Plato*, Jowett's translation, vol. IV, 377.
5. Adapted from Hugo Winckler, *Die babylonische Geisteskultur in ihren Beziehungen zur Kulturentwicklung der Menschheit* (Leipzig, 1907), 122–24.
6. Sir Leonard Woolley, *Ur: The First Phases* (London and New York: Penguin Books, 1946).

THE EXPRESSION OF MYTH IN DANCE IMAGES (1978)

1. [This article first appeared in *Dance as Cultural Heritage, Volume I: Selected Papers from the ADG–CORD Conference 1978*. ADG stands for American Dance Guild. CORD stands for Congress on Research in Dance. These two professional organizations were founded in New York City in 1956 and 1965, respectively, and they are still operating. They often hold their annual conferences jointly. The article included the following note from the editors:

"This Introduction closely follows Professor Campbell's remarks at the Conference session on The Expression of Myth in Dance Images. His remarks were tape-recorded at that time and later transcribed for publication. As a part of this session, Lakshmi Shanmukham, the distinguished Indian dancer, with her orchestra, presented an item from the repertoire of Bharata Natyam, which interpreted a sung poetic text on the theme of Shiva."]

2. [Campbell was obviously referring to the twentieth century.]

3. [The Daśarūpa written by the Indian aesthetic philosopher known as Dhanamjaya is widely regarded as one of the most complete texts on Indian theater, which includes dance, drama, and music. Written somewhere between the fourth and sixth centuries A.D., it was discovered by Western aesthetic philosophers in the late nineteenth century and translated into English in 1912 by George Haas. A fuller discussion of the Daśarūpa may be found in Campbell, *Inner Reaches of Outer Space*, 138–42 (see foreword, n. 5).]

4. [It is interesting to note that this theme, which Campbell noticed as appearing more frequently in the late 1970s, continues to appear ever more frequently now, especially in popular films and literature, from *Thelma and Louise* to *Frozen* and *The Hunger Games*, as women have continued to enter the "fields of action proper to the male."]

5. [One wonders here why Campbell did not mention Graham's *Diversion of Angels*, a masterwork of American modern dance on the theme of love. Perhaps more than any other Graham work, this lyrical and abstract dance is created purely from the "form and sweep" of the dynamic pulsating rhythms of Graham's dance technique, the one that so arrested Campbell when he first saw it at Bennington College in 1937 and which he describes so enthusiastically in "Betwixt the Cup and the Lip."

For more information see: Anna Kisselgoff, "A Classical Approach to the Graham Karma," *New York Times*, October 26, 1999.]

6. References for this chapter: Adolf Bastian, *Das Beständige in den Menschenrassen* (Berlin: Dietrich Reimer, 1868); *Coomaraswamy: Selected Papers*, 2 vols., ed. Roger Lipsey (Princeton, NJ: Princeton University Press, 1977), vol. I, 13–42; Edward C. Dimock Jr., "Doctrine and Practice among Vaiṣṇavas of Bengal," in *Krishna: Myths, Rites, and Attitudes*, ed. Milton Singer (Honolulu: East-West Center Press, 1966), 41–63; George C. O. Haas, ed. and trans., *The Dásarupa (The Ten Forms [of Drama])* (Delhi: Motilal Banarsidass, 1962); and the 1978 summer Asian Conference, Honolulu.

Part II: Mythology and Form in the Performing and Visual Arts

Chapter 1

1. [For a more in-depth discussion of the relationship between mythology and biology, see Joseph Campbell, *The Masks of God: Creative Mythology* (New York: Viking Press, 1968), 625–46.]
2. This is the essential point brought out some years ago by Ananda K. Coomaraswamy in his important articles "The Philosophy of Mediaeval and Oriental Art," first published in *Zalmoxis* I (1938). These have been reissued in Roger Lipsey, ed., *Coomaraswamy*, 2 vols., Bollingen Series LXXXIX (Princeton, NJ: Princeton University Press, 1977); see vol. 2, p. 52, citing Thomas Aquinas, *Summa Theologica* I.117.1.

Chapter 2

1. Karl Nierendorf, *Paul Klee: Paintings and Watercolors, 1913 to 1939* (New York: Oxford University Press, 1941), 25–26.
2. Ibid., 23.
3. Quoted by G. di San Lazzaro, *Klee: A Study of His Life and Work* (New York: Frederick A. Praeger, 1957), 18.
4. Johann Peter Eckermann, *Gespräche mit Goethe*, ed. Eduard Castle, vol. 1 (Berlin: Deutsches Verlagshaus Bong & Co., 1916), 251.

Chapter 3

1. Robert Descharnes, *The World of Salvador Dali* (New York and Evanston: Harper and Row, 1962), 142.

Chapter 4

1. Wagner himself, as he describes in his autobiography, had for a time considered the possibility of a Buddhist opera.
2. The play was produced, also, in New York, at the old Century Theater on 62nd Street and Central Park West.
3. John Balance, "The Berlin Theatre," *The Mask* 1, no. 9 (November 1908), 175–77; and again, John Semar, "The Return of Gordon Craig to England," *The Mask* 4, no. 2 (October, 1911), 81–82.
4. Gordon Craig, "The Artist and Nature, An Extract Translated from the Conversations of Goethe as Recorded by Eckermann. 1822–1832," *The Mask* 4, no. 4 (October 1912), 181.

CHAPTER 5

1. Summarized from Helen Caldwell, *Michio Ito: The Dancer and His Dances* (Berkeley and Los Angeles: University of California Press, 1977), 37–41.

2. W. B. Yeats, *Essays and Introductions* (New York: Collier Books, 1961), 224.

3. Ibid., 339.

4. Ibid., 38.

5. Émile Jaques-Dalcroze, *Rhythm, Music and Education*, trans. Harold F. Rubinstein (New York and London: Putnam, 1921), 244; cited by Caldwell, *Michio Ito*, 4.

6. Ananda K. Coomaraswamy, "Introduction to the Art of Eastern Asia," in Roger Lipsey, ed., *Coomaraswamy*, 2 vols. (Princeton: Princeton University Press, 1977), vol. 1, 111.

7. Coomaraswamy, "The Intellectual Operation in Indian Art," in Lipsey, *Coomaraswamy*, 131, citing *Śukranītisāra* 4.70–71.

8. James Joyce, *A Portrait of the Artist as a Young Man* (New York: Viking Compass Editions, 1964), 205–6.

   [A fuller discussion of the Joycean concept of aesthetic arrest and its relationship to Dante, Wagner, Schopenhauer, and Hindu Buddhist philosophy can be found in Campbell, *Masks of God*, 67–75 (see chap. 7, n. 2), and also in Campbell, *Inner Reaches of Outer Space*, 122–35 (see foreword, n. 5).]

CHAPTER 6

1. Caldwell, *Michio Ito*, 37–54 (see chap. 5, n. 1).

2. Ibid., 48.

3. Yeats, *Essays and Introductions*, 221–24 (see chap. 5, n. 2).

4. Quoted by Caldwell, *Michio Ito*, 50.

5. Ibid., 54.

6. Ibid., 226.

7. James W. Flannery, *W. B. Yeats and the Idea of a Theatre* (Toronto: Macmillan of Canada, 1976), 266.

CHAPTER 7

1. Isadora Duncan, *The Art of the Dance*, edited with an introduction by Sheldon Cheney (New York: Theater Arts, 1928), 126; from an essay,

"Dancing in Relation to Religion and Love," first published in *Theatre Arts Monthly* (1927).

2. Ibid., 68; from an essay, "The Dancer and Nature," written in Germany about 1905.

3. Ibid., 64–65; from a fragment written in a notebook of her first Athens period.

4. [Although this explanation by Isadora on the origin of her dance is well known, and often quoted, writer Peter Kurth, in his exhaustive biography, points out that Isadora's grandparents did not cross the plains in a covered wagon. They arrived, as the wealthier gold prospectors did, by ship through Panama. See Peter Kurth, *Isadora: A Sensational Life* (Boston, Little Brown & Company 2001), 6.]

5. Duncan, *Art of the Dance*, 47–48; "I See America Dancing," first published in the *New-York Herald-Tribune*, October 2, 1927.

6. John Martin, *America Dancing* (New York: Dodge Publishing Company, 1936), 158, without reference to source.

7. See above, p. 98

8. [Campbell's reference here is undocumented. It is possible that he is referring to a 1910 incident reported in the *New York Times* (January 9, 1910), when police discovered Isadora's nephew, Manalkas, in Greek classical dress on the streets of New York and promptly took him to the Children's Aid Society. Or is it possible that Campbell himself, in New York in the late 1930s, saw Isadora's brother, Raymond, and his family, on one of their visits from Paris, emerge from a subway train on Sixth Avenue in full Greek classical dress?]

9. Joyce, *Portrait*, 241 (see chap. 5, n. 8).

CHAPTER 8

1. Martin, *America Dancing*, 51–53 (see chap. 7, n. 6).

2. Ibid., 22–23: "Isadora" by Margharita Duncan.

CHAPTER 9

1. Oswald Spengler, *The Decline of the West*, trans. Charles Francis Atkinson (New York: Alfred A. Knopf, vol. I, 1926, vol. II, 1928), vol. II: 117.

2. Duncan, *Art of the Dance*, 138 (see chap. 7, n. 1).

   [Isadora's comments here certainly imply that her dances were moments of "enraptured spontaneity," as Campbell called them in chapter 7. However, a renaissance of Duncan's work in the late twentieth century initiated by a 1977 performance of the Isadora

Duncan Centenary Company, founded by Julia Levien and Hortense Kooluris, began a significant reexamination of the choreographer's work that questions this interpretation.

Between them, Levien and Kooluris had studied and performed with Elizabeth Duncan, Isadora's sister, and Anna and Irma Duncan, two of Duncan's adopted daughters, who performed and taught with her as the Isadorables throughout Europe, Russia, and the United States. Irma was also the author of *The Technique of Isadora Duncan*, which includes a series of exercises requiring precise use of body parts, rhythm, dynamics, and shape.

In 1978, Kooluris and Levien renamed their company the Isadora Duncan Commemorative Dance Company, and through it they trained an entire generation of dancers, including Lori Belilove, Julie Bresciani, Kathleen Quinlan, Catherine Gallant, and others who continue teaching Duncan technique, performing and staging her dances to this day. In her obituary of Levien, *New York Times* dance critic Jennifer Dunning said that she helped to "prove that Duncan choreographed rather than improvised dances, and that they had structure, set steps, gestures and patterns, all informed by a philosophy of naturally flowing and gravity-bound movement."

Whether Campbell was aware of the Duncan renaissance is not known. I never heard him speak about it. Irma Duncan's book was part of Erdman's personal library that I catalogued in 2000 as part of the gift of the Jean Erdman Papers to the Jerome Robbins Dance Research Collection at the NYPL for the Performing Arts at Lincoln Center.

Whether Duncan's dances were precisely structured or "enraptured spontaneity," all scholars, as well as reviewers and anecdotal reports of people who saw her perform, attest to the Dionysian quality of her dance.

For more information see www.isadoraduncanarchive.org; Ann Daly, "The Natural Body," in *Moving History / Dancing Cultures*, eds. Ann Dils and Ann Cooper Albright (Middletown, CT: Wesleyan University Press, 2001); Irma Duncan, *The Technique of Isadora Duncan* (New York: Kamin Publishers, 1937); Jennifer Dunning, "Julia Levien, 94, Authority on the Dances of Isadora Duncan, Dies," *New York Times*, September 9, 2006.]

3. *New York Times*, November 19, 1916, section II, 6, cited by Caldwell, *Michio Ito*, 57 (see chap. 5, n. 1).

4. Caldwell, *Michio Ito*, 77, citing Ted Shawn, *Thirty-Three Years of*

American Dance, 1927–1959, and *The American Ballet* (Pittsfield, MA: privately printed, 1959), 13.

5. *Musical Courier*, November 3, 1927, 40; cited by Caldwell, *Michio Ito*, 98.

6. Caldwell, *Michio Ito*, 86.

7. [John Martin, dance critic at the *New York Times* from 1927 to 1962 was another important champion and midwife of the American modern dance movement. His carefully crafted reviews form another body of literature of the period. *Dance Magazine*, which began publishing in 1927 as *The American Dancer*, was also witness to the birth of the movement, although its editorial slant was more of a trade magazine, and it tended to give greater coverage to ballet and Broadway dance.]

CHAPTER 10

1. [Laban called his notation method Kinetographie in the first public documentation of the system published in 1928 in the magazine *Schrifttanz*. Labanotation is the name used in the United States and England today. It is known as Kinetography Laban throughout much of Europe and South America.]

2. [The "twelve primary directions" Campbell refers to here are the twelve vertices, or corners of the three cardinal planes: vertical, sagittal, and horizontal. These three planes form the inner architecture of the icosahedron, a twenty-faceted Platonic solid. Laban used the five Platonic solids as scaffoldings to observe and describe movement in space. Within his framework, known as Choreutics, or Space Harmony, upon which Labanotation is based, the octahedron and the cube are equally important primary spatial scaffolding models.

The inner architecture of the octahedron is the *dimensional* cross of axes, again, vertical, horizontal, and sagittal. These three straight, central pathways with a common midpoint connect the six spatial directions: up, down, forward, backward, right, and left. Throughout the Laban literature, one finds the six spatial directions of the cross of axes referred to as the "primary" spatial directions because all of the other spatial directions are created from them, much as variations in pigments are formed from the three primary colors: red, blue, and yellow.

The inner architecture of the cube is the *diagonal* cross of axes; four straight, central pathways with a common midpoint, connecting the eight spatial directions toward the vertices, or corners, of the cube. These are known as Right Forward High, Left Back Low, Left Forward High, Right Back Low, Left Back High, Right Forward Low, Right

Back High, and Left Forward Low. The eight spatial directions of the cube combined with the six directions of the octahedron, and the twelve directions of the three planes that Campbell mentioned equal twenty-six spatial directions that are also often referred to in the Laban literature as the "primary" directions of spatial form.

The three planes were a favorite spatial scaffolding of the pioneering and post-pioneering generations of American modern dance. One can find many examples of movement into the twelve spatial directions encompassed by the planes, as well as movement using planar counter tensions, in their choreography. However, these twelve spatial directions are not referred to as the "primary" spatial directions in the Laban literature.

Whether or not Laban, the product of a classical education and strongly influenced by the mystical teachings of Rosicrucianism, was aware of the spiritual attributes of Pythagorean geometry, and therefore the movement he and his followers created and notated using the Platonic solids as a spatial framework, remains a matter of much discussion among Laban scholars.

For further information about Laban's theories of Space Harmony, see Carol-Lynne Moore, *The Harmonic Structure of Movement, Music, and Dance According to Rudolf Laban* (Lewiston, NY: Edwin Mellen Press, 2009); Valerie Preston-Dunlop, *Rudolf Laban: An Extraordinary Life* (Hampshire, UK: Dance Books, 1998), 10–12; and Rudolf von Laban, *Choreutics* (London: Macdonald & Evans, 1966).]

3. A sequence composed in 1925: 1. Ceremonial Figure, 2. Masked Figure, 3. Spectre, and in 1926, 4. Witch Dance.

4. The first of the *Sequence of Visions*, to which this Witch Dance was to be the fourth.

5. The seventh member of a sequence of group dances composed in 1920–23: 1. Prelude, 2. Dance of Longing, 3. Dance of Love, 4. Dance of Lust, 5. Dance of Sorrow, 6. Dance of the Demon, 7. Dance of Death, 8. Dance of Life.

6. Mary Wigman, *The Language of Dance*, trans. Walter Sorell (Middletown, CT: Wesleyan University Press, 1966), 40–42.

7. Ibid., 90–95.

8. Ibid., 96.

9. Ibid., 97.

10. Hanya Holm, "The German Dance in the American Scene," in *Modern Dance*, ed. Virginia Stewart (New York: E. Weyke, 1935), 129–33, abridged.

CHAPTER 11

1. See above, page 74.

2. Martha Graham, "Platform for the American Dance," a program note to *Martha Graham and Dance Group* (New York: Artcraft Litho. 9, Printing Company, no date), 1.

3. Ibid., 2.

4. [While Graham openly acknowledged her debt to Campbell in her 1991 autobiography *Blood Memory*, excerpts from a letter written by Erdman to Campbell when she was touring with the company in 1939 reveal just how much both she and Louis Horst were seeking that help:

"I have found out why Martha is always interested to hear me speak of you. In the first place I think she is genuinely interested in our whole relationship because it somehow touches her personal life...but the reason she always pricks up her ears if I say anything about your opinions is that she really senses somehow that you could be a great help....

"Louie [Horst] put me on the spot at dinner on the train last evening by saying to me (Martha, Nina [Fonaroff], Louie and at table) 'Does Joe still dislike the document [*American Document*, a full-length dance choreographed by Graham] & think the words are all wrong etc.'—Poor Martha was embarrassed & I nearly died but tried to get around the thing by saying as little as possible. I finally muttered something about your having seen it as a 'good show' in Carnegie, the second time—you see—Oh dear! I explained to Martha that you had expected the movement to be an illustration of the words & that the second time you saw it in Martha's terms—& it was a 'good show'—[w]ell she looked a touch crest-fallen at that last—and then took up the conversation herself saying, as if I had said to her in so many words that you had not believed in the dance as Americana—that she knew the document was a 'good show' but that it was not right—It was representational art. She said she knew that it was too conscious, the use of historical incident, & of folk material, was too conscious—that she knew someday there would be a dance which would not depend upon incident at all—but which would arise of its own accord & spontaneously from the land—unconscious of its use of American material—But that before such a dance could be made a whole psychological change was needed—she said we had to return to the 'things' which the East (Orient) has known for centuries (!)

"Furthermore, that she did not know whether she would be the one ever to do such a dance. She knew the 'thing' was just around the corner but as yet she could not grasp it and the only way she knew to get at the 'thing' was by restatement of our legends & rituals first—because this art must be based on ritual, not necessarily religion but some ritual belonging to the American people—'Our ritual,' she said, 'is our life.'"]

5. [While it is true that Cunningham had been deeply inspired by Cage's composition course at the Cornish School of the Arts (now Cornish College of the Arts) in Seattle, he didn't actually come with Cage to New York. Cunningham arrived in New York in 1939 at the invitation of Martha Graham, who had seen him in class at Cornish. Cage arrived in New York with his wife, Xenia Kashevaroff, in the spring of 1942, following the critical success of his commissioned score for the CBS radio play *The City Wears a Slouch Hat*.

Amazingly, Campbell had met Kashevaroff in 1932 during his maritime adventure with Ed Ricketts along the northwest coast from Washington to Alaska. The daughter of a Russian Orthodox priest (who conducted mass in Russian and Tlingit, a Native American language), the exotic and alluring Kashevaroff and the dashing, young Campbell formed an intimate and lasting friendship. In the next five years, Campbell, Cage, Cunningham, Erdman, and Kashevaroff would form various relationships as friends, collaborators, and colleagues. See David Vaughan, *Merce Cunningham: Fifty Years*, ed. Melissa Harris (Reading, PA: Aperture, 1997), 20–22; Richard Kostelanetz, *Conversing with Cage*, 2nd ed. (New York: Routledge, 2003), 11; and Larsen, *Fire in the Mind*, 206–9 (see foreword, n. 1).]

6. [The School of American Ballet (SAB) was founded by philanthropists Lincoln Kirstein and Edward Warburg with the Georgian-Russian choreographer George Balanchine. While Kirstein was certainly an essential partner in the founding, development, and promotion of SAB, Balanchine's now famous edict, "But first, a school!"—which is how he replied to Kirstein's invitation to establish the company that would eventually become the New York City Ballet—demonstrates Balanchine's artistic and pedagogical hegemony over the institution. It was Balanchine's groundbreaking Neoclassical ballet technique and aesthetic that Cunningham imbibed at SAB.]

7. [While it may seem obvious, it is important to note that both Cunningham and Erdman were also trained in Graham technique. Cunningham studied it under Bonnie Bird at Cornish, while Erdman learned it directly from Graham and various members of her company at Sarah Lawrence. Both of them took Graham technique classes at the Bennington Summer School of the Dance. It's also more than interesting to note in relation to Campbell's aesthetic philosophy that despite Graham's well-developed technique, she worked with her solo performers, as many

choreographers do, by suggesting ideas for which the dancers themselves created movement material that she then shaped to suit her vision. Erdman often spoke to me with a secret pride about how she had "choreographed all her own parts" in *Letter to the World*. See Vaughan, *Merce Cunningham*, 23; and Emiko Tokunaga, *Yuriko: An American Japanese Dancer: To Wash in the Rain and Polish with the Wind* (Tokunaga Dance Ko., 2008), 82.]

CHAPTER 12

1. [Memories differ as to who actually suggested the duet concert. Whether it was Cage or Campbell, it seems clear that both men wanted to encourage the choreographic development of their respective partners. Actually, Cage was still married to Xenia Kashevaroff at this point. Some scholars speculate that his psychological turmoil regarding his sexual orientation was the theme of his work for the Cunningham/Erdman duet.

   For more information see *Dance and Myth: The World of Jean Erdman: Part 1* (see foreword, n. 15); and Gerald Paul Cox, "Collaged Codes: John Cage's Credo in Us," (doctoral thesis, Case Western Reserve University, 2011), http://rave.ohiolink.edu/etdc/view?acc_num=case1301 716791.]

2. [The concert evolved over a period of several years. For her part, Erdman had begun *The Transformations of Medusa* several years earlier in response to an assignment on the archaic two-dimensional style in Louis Horst's composition class. She began with a purely physical exploration of the style, asking, "What kind of person would move like this?" She worked on the first section of the dance for a whole year, looking for the psychological basis of the style. She discovered that it was that of a "fanatic," someone with a "single focus." It was Campbell who, during one of his visits to Erdman's studio, saw the dance character as Medusa and suggested she call it Gorgoneion, providing the mythological grounding for the work (Campbell/Erdman letters, July 1941). Erdman performed Gorgoneion in a 1941 concert of Erick Hawkins's work in which she appeared as a guest artist. She developed the second and third sections of the dance over the succeeding year guided by the mythological structuring Campbell had elucidated.

   The first incarnation of the duet concert with Cunningham was during the summer of 1942 at what was by then called the Bennington College Summer Dance Session. There, Erdman performed all three sections of *The Transformations of Medusa* with its commissioned score by Louis Horst. Cunningham performed *Renaissance Testimonials* with music by Maxwell Powers. Together they performed three duets: the two that Campbell describes and *Seeds of Brightness* with a commissioned score by Norman Lloyd. This concert also included solos choreographed and performed by Nina Fonaroff, another Graham dancer.

The trio repeated their efforts in a shared concert presented by the *Dance Observer* at Doris Humphrey and Charles Weidman's Studio Theater in October 1942. On this concert, Cunningham premiered *Totem Ancestor*. Both Erdman and Cunningham continued to develop their work to arrive at the program Campbell describes for the Chicago concert in 1943.

For further information see *Dance and Myth: The World of Jean Erdman: Part 1* (see foreword, n. 15); Cox, "Collaged Codes: John Cage's Credo"; Elizabeth McPherson, ed., *The Bennington School of the Dance: A History in Writings and Interviews* (Jefferson, NC: McFarland and Company, 2013), appendix A; and Vaughan, *Merce Cunningham*, 26, 286 (see chap. 11, n. 5).]

3. [The original handwritten version of the score by Cage, found in Erdman's personal archives, states that the work is for "contralto and percussion (two large tom toms and a large cymbal)." The singer chants the text of Cummings's poem. At several points Erdman also spoke the poem.]

4. [According to Cage, Campbell commissioned him to create the music. Erdman told me that Cage stayed in her apartment in lieu of payment for the music. A letter from Erdman to Campbell in July 1942 reveals that Cage told Erdman that he was unable to create the music for the concert because Max Ernst and Peggy Guggenheim were kicking him and Xenia out of their apartment. He didn't have a job and needed to find both a place to stay and a means of support. Erdman immediately offered to let him and Xenia live in the Greenwich Village apartment during the summer of 1942, which had a baby grand piano at the time, so that he could finish the music. Erdman was either touring with Graham or up in Bennington. Campbell was spending the summer in a rented room near the Bennington campus, but Erdman was a bit wary that he would agree to the arrangement.

The title *Credo in US* appears variously in published materials; as Campbell wrote it with "U.S.," as *Credo in US*, which is the way it appears in the chronology in David Vaughan's *Merce Cunningham* (see chap. 11, n. 5) and as *Credo in Us* in Richard Kostelanetz's *Conversing with Cage*, 2nd ed. (New York, London: Routledge, 2003). In the program from the Art Club of Chicago, it appears as *Credo in US*, whereas on the program for the Bennington concert, it appears as *Credo in Us*.

While the dance was never performed again after the 1943 performance in Chicago, the musical work was a breakthrough in Cage's musical development and is still performed frequently today. A more detailed history and analysis of the work, including the various versions of the title, can be found in Cox, "Collaged Codes: John Cage's Credo" (see chap. 12, n. 1).]

5. [According to various sources, Graham and Hawkins were married in 1948 and separated in 1950 or 1951. For further information see Martha Graham, *Blood Memory* (New York: Washington Square Press Publication, 1991), 171–78; and Anna Kisselgoff, "Martha Graham Dies at 96: A Revolutionary in Dance," *New York Times*, April 2, 1991.]

6. [According to Renata Celichowska, a dance historian and former member of the Erick Hawkins Dance Company, *Here and Now with Watchers* premiered in 1957. This is also the year that is generally attributed to the debut of the Erick Hawkins Dance Company. See Renata Celichowska, "Erick Hawkins," Dance Heritage Coalition (2012), http://www.danceheritage.org/treasures/hawkins_essay_celichowska.pdf; and Selma Jeanne Cohen, *The Modern Dance: Seven Statements of Belief* (Middletown, CT: Wesleyan University Press, 1965), 105.]

7. [What Cunningham was doing in his technique, which Campbell aptly describes as "dexterous and difficult," and in his groundbreaking choreographic aesthetic, which eschewed story, character development, spatial hierarchies, and musical form, would inspire generations of artists and audiences. That Campbell seemed to find the profound effect of Cunningham's choices hard to discern is hardly surprising, for as dance historian Don McDonagh notes, "Cunningham was speaking the language of his creative time almost before the time was aware that a new choreographic language was needed." See Don McDonagh, *The Rise and Fall and Rise of Modern Dance* (New York: Outerbridge & Dienstfrey, 1970), 54.]

8. [The "world study-tour" to which Campbell refers was actually a trip around the world that Erdman took in lieu of her senior year at Sarah Lawrence College. She went with her recently retired father, mother, and younger sister Marjorie (also then a student at Sarah Lawrence College). The "study" portion was provided by Professor Campbell, whose letters were waiting for the young Erdman at each port of call along the journey. The voluminous correspondence between the two, recounted in *A Fire in the Mind*, traces their growing passion and influence on each other's ideas concerning aesthetics, myth, and psychology. See Larsen, *Fire in the Mind*, 249–69 (see foreword, n. 1).]

9. Friedrich Nietzsche, *The Will to Power*, par. 818.
10. [Campbell doesn't cite the reference for this quote. While I could not find it verbatim, it is the essence of her aesthetic philosophy and can be found in some variation in almost every article she wrote and interview that she gave.

    For more information see Jean Erdman, "Young Dancers State Their Views as Told to Joseph Campbell," *Dance Observer* (April 1948); Jean Erdman, "The Dance as a Non-Verbal Poetical Image," part 2, *Dance Observer* (May 1949); and Jean Erdman, "A Contemporary Dancer Looks at Her Heritage," part 2, *Dance Magazine* (December 1960).]
11. Friedrich Nietzsche, *Ecce Homo*, par. 4.

CHAPTER 13

1. Joyce, *Portrait*, 214 (see chap. 5, n. 8).
2. [While Campbell may have felt that the absence of men in Manhattan during World War II was an inspiration for Erdman's trio, I never heard her speak of it in those terms. I learned the dance and performed it with her in the summer of 1977, dancing the role of the Youthful Virgin, the role she originally choreographed for herself, while she, sixty-one at the time, danced the Mothering Aspect. Over the more than twenty-five years that I performed and staged the work, I had many conversations with her about the inspiration, content, and form of this beautiful and intricate dance.

    She did mention the work of the British classical scholar and feminist Jane Harrison on the Cretan goddess religion as a starting point for her musings about the dance. From time to time she would relate Campbell's version of the origin of the dance with affectionate humor. In Erdman's version, captured in her own words and voice in part 1 of the video series *Dance and Myth: The World of Jean Erdman*, she says that the dance is "the story of what is inside us as women."

    As with many of Erdman's dances, Campbell provided the title for this trio, after it was completed, from his deep fount of mythological references. Perhaps it was Campbell's own sensitivity to the lack of testosterone that inspired his title, or perhaps he saw the synchronicity of Erdman's choosing this theme at this time as similar to the kind of sensitivity to psychological zeitgeist he ascribes to Picasso.

    To understand Erdman's creative process in this dance, it's important to know that she did not create the movement to a previously composed score by Cage. She created the movement in silence, working alone in the studio to discover the dynamic rhythm and shape of the movement appropriate to each of the three aspects of the feminine principle portrayed in the dance: the Mothering Aspect, Youthful Virgin, and Woman of Experience. Cage visited Erdman's rehearsals and noted the count structures she had created for each section. He then created his score in reference to these count structures and whatever qualitative inspiration he may have drawn from Erdman's movement.

For further information see *Dance and Myth: The World of Jean Erdman, Part 1* (see foreword, n. 15); and Deborah Welsh, with Jean Erdman, Nancy Allison, and Leslie Dillingham, "Journeys of Body and Soul: Jean Erdman's Dances" in *C. G. Jung and the Humanities: Toward a Hermeneutics of Culture*, eds. Karin Barnaby and Pellegrino D'Acierno (Princeton, NJ: Princeton University Press, 1990), 217–29.]

3. [This is the University of Colorado at Boulder.]

4. [In our conversations, as Erdman taught me *Passage* in 1986, she described the dance, created in 1946 at the same time that she was working on *Ophelia*, as an antidote to the unrelenting physical and psychic stress she experienced while working on the dismemberment of *Ophelia*. For her, *Ophelia* began as an abstract image of an unsuccessful threshold crossing, whereas *Passage* was an equally abstract image of a successful crossing. In her narration for part 1 of the video series *Dance and Myth*, she describes it as an abstract image of "a leap through the threshold of life."

Campbell and Erdman had a morning ritual of breakfasting together, in which he would read to her everything he had written the day before. In 1946, he was deeply involved in writing the manuscript that would become *The Hero with a Thousand Faces*, his exegesis of the monomyth, the cycle of psychological events that characterizes the "actualization of destiny in time" found in myths and legends throughout the world. In Campbell's theory, a successful threshold crossing is a key event in the cycle.

For a more in-depth discussion of the stages of the hero's journey, see Campbell, *The Hero with a Thousand Faces.*

5. [Campbell's description of the creative process for *Solstice* seems somewhat different than Erdman's perspective. In Erdman's recollections, documented in part 2 of the video series *Dance and Myth*, the process was initiated by a playful discussion between the two, where Campbell suggested that the permutations of the infinity symbol could offer a variety of floor patterns suitable for a group dance. That idea combined with Erdman's concurrent inspiration from Jane Harrison's writing on the Cretan art and ritual was the genesis of this celebratory dance.

Dyer's masks were created more or less simultaneously with Erdman's choreography. At a benefit event to raise funds for the video series *Dance and Myth* at Marymount Manhattan College in New York in June 1989, Donald McKayle and Merce Cunningham recalled with affection and laughter the difficulties they each had performing the choreography when they first had to do it while wearing the masks.

For more information see *Benefit for Jean Erdman Video Archive Project*, phase 2, disc 3, Jerome Robbins Dance Research Collection, New York Public Library (call number: MGZTL4-1539).]

6. [Campbell was, in fact, in India during the time of Erdman's performances and acted as her agent there. Jean also revealed to me that Joe was often her stage manager for these performances, so he had a very firsthand experience of what it was like to present a dance concert in the heat of India!

For more information see Larsen, *Fire in the Mind*, 370–88 (see foreword, n. 1).]

7. [It's interesting to note here that, according to Erdman in conversation with me, Laderman was inspired to create *Duet for Flute and Dancer* after seeing the inventive way in which she interacted with Debussy's score for *Syrinx*, the flute solo that Erdman used as the accompaniment for *Hamadryad*, which she had choreographed in 1948. Laderman and Erdman's collaboration was the subject of "Scoring for the Dancer," an article that appeared in *Time* magazine (April 1, 1957).]

8. [Of course, as Campbell's wife, Erdman was already well-acquainted with *Finnegans Wake*. Campbell was working with his Sarah Lawrence colleague Henry Morton Robinson on their book *A Skeleton Key to Finnegans Wake* from 1938, the year that Campbell and Erdman married, through 1944, the year the book was published.

For more information about the genesis of *The Coach with the Six Insides*, see Larsen, *Fire in the Mind*, 450–52 (see foreword, n. 1).]

9. Yeats, *Essays and Introductions*, 221–22 (see chap. 5, n. 2).

10. Michael Feingold, *Village Voice*, February 22, 1979. The review continues: "In those days, its artistic materials were unusual. Now that so many of its devices and juxtapositions have become common property, it is ahead of its time in a different way. The audience is not menaced, confronted, spatially involved, or insulted; there is no nudity and no deafening rock music; the vocal effects do not include any screaming or any stylized speech that distorts the sense of the words; the actors all appear to be well trained sentient beings; although there are many pictorial effects, there has been no attempt on the director's part to make the

cast seem two-dimensional or turn them into animated objects. Most experimental of all, the piece is intended to engage the intellect, not the viscera."

11. James George Frazer, *The Golden Bough: a Study in Magic and Religion* (New York: Macmillan, 1922), 469.

12. John Layard, *The Stone Men of Malekula* (London: Chatto & Windus, 1942).

13. Ovid, *Metamorphoses*, XV, trans. Frank Justus Miller, Loeb Classical Library (Cambridge, MA: Harvard University Press, 1916), 165–72.

14. *Bhagavad Gita*, trans. Swami Nikhilananda (New York: Ramakrishna-Vivekananda Center, 1944), 2.22–23.

15. Joyce, *Finnegans Wake*, 151 (see "Betwixt the Cup and the Lip," n. 2).

16. E. A. W. Budge, trans., *The Per-em-hrw, or Day of Putting Forth*, commonly called *The Book of the Dead*, reissued in *The Sacred Books and Early Literature of the East*, vol. II, ed. Charles F. Horne (New York and London: Parke, Austin, and Lipscomb, 1917), 196–97.

17. Katha Upaniṣad, 1.2.22 and 1.3.12.

18. [For a more in-depth treatment of the meaning of the sacred sound OM, see Joseph Campbell, *The Mythic Image*, Bollingen Series C (Princeton, NJ: Princeton University Press, 1974), 356–92.]

19. [As many directors and performing artists will probably note, since the early 1970s when Erdman was creating *Moon Mysteries*, many performers are now equally accomplished as actors, dancers, and musicians, plus a host of increasingly specialized skills, such as skateboarding, aerial dancing, and American Sign Language, to name just a few.]

20. Yeats, "Certain Noble Plays of Japan," in *Essays and Introductions*, 221 (see chap. 5, n. 2).

21. Oswald Spengler, *The Decline of the West*, vol. I, 193, n. 3 (see chap. 9, n. 1).

22. Ibid, 194.

ILLUSTRATION SOURCES AND
PERMISSION ACKNOWLEDGMENTS

———————●———————

Figure 1: Modern dance (South Korea, 2009). Photograph by the Korean Culture and Information Service, used through a Creative Commons license.

Figure 2: Dance instructor (United States, 1943). "Daytona Beach, Florida. Bethune-Cookman College. Instructor showing steps in a modern dance class" by Gordon Parks, from the U.S. Farm Security Administration — Office of War Information Photograph Collection / Library of Congress. Public domain.

Figure 3: Martha Graham (United States, 1945). Photograph by Barbara Morgan (1900–92) / Private Collection / Underwood Archives/ UIG / Bridgeman Images. Used with permission.

Figure 4: Anna Duncan (United States, 1921). "Long Beach, Long Island, New York," a glass transparency by Arnold Genthe (1869–1942). Public domain.

Figure 5: Untitled drawing by Paul Klee (watercolor and pencil on paper, Germany, c. 1914). From a private Collection / Bridgeman Images. Used with permission.

Figure 6: "Greek" dancers (United States, c. 1920). "Group of girls in Greek dance" by Underwood and Underwood / Library of Congress. Public domain.

Figure 7: Hula dancers (United States, c. 1901). "Pretty Hula Girls, Honolulu, Hawaii" by B. L. Singley; Keystone View Company / Library of Congress. Public domain.

Figure 8: Dancers (United States, 1939). "Jitterbugging in Negro juke joint, Saturday evening, outside Clarksdale, Mississippi" by Marion

Post Walcott (1910–90) for the U.S. Works Progress Administration /
Library of Congress. Public domain.

Figure 9: "The World" (Italy, 1865). Tarot card by F. F. Solesi (Wikimedia
Commons).

Figure 10: Śiva Naṭarāja (bronze, India, eleventh century). "Shiva as Lord of
Dance (Nataraja)" was a gift of R. H. Ellsworth Ltd. to the Metropoli-
tan Museum of Art, in honor of Susan Dillon, 1987. Used through a
Creative Commons (public domain) license.

Figures 11 and 12: Andaman islanders (Myanmar, c. 1906–8). Photograph by
A. R. Radcliffe-Brown. Published in *The Andaman Islanders: A Study
in Social Anthropology* (Cambridge, UK: Cambridge University Press,
1922). Public domain.

Figure 13: *Ojibwa Snowshoe Dance* by George Catlin (United States, 1835).
"Ancient Ojibwa Tradition: The Snowshoe Dance, performed at the first
snowfall every year since time immemorial." Wikimedia Commons.

Figure 14: Hula dancer teaching audience (United States, 2013). Photo by
Lance Cheung for U.S. Department of Agriculture / Library of Congress. Public domain.

Figure 15: *Dōjōji* by Ippitsusai Bunchō (ink on paper, Japan, c. 1771).
"Ichimura Uzaemon IX in the Role of Kiyohime in Musume Dōjōji
(the Girl of Dōjōji)." Used with permission of the Metropolitan Museum of Art through a Creative Commons (public domain) license.

Figure 16: Kiyohime transforms into a serpent (ink on paper, Japan, c.
1400). "Kiyohime" — artist unknown. Wikimedia Commons.

Figure 17: Martha Graham in *El Penitente* (United States, 1940). Photog-
rapher unknown. Reproduced with permission of Martha Graham
Resources, a division of the Martha Graham Center of Contemporary
Dance, www.marthagraham.org.

Figure 18: Radha and Kṛṣṇa (ink on paper, India, c. 1780). "Radha and
Krishna as Lovers, from the 'Gitagovinda' series" was a gift of John
and Berthe Ford, 2001, to the Walters Art Museum. Used through a
Creative Commons license.

Figure 19: *Tristan and Isolt* by George Alfred Williams (print, United States,
1909). From Richard La Galliene, *Wagner's Tristan and Isolde* (New
York: Frederick A. Stokes Company, 1909). Internet Archive / public
domain.

Figure 20: Śiva Naṭarāja (bronze, India). Photo by Elena Vakhnik /
Shutterstock.

Figure 21: Nijinsky in *L'Après-midi d'un faune* (France, 1912). "Nijinsky as
faun in the premiere of ballet *L'Après-midi d'un faune*." Photograph by

Adolph de Meyer, May 29, 1912. From *La Prelude a l'Après-midi d'un faune* (Paris: Paul Iribe, 1914). Wikimedia Commons.

Figure 22: *Herakles the Archer* by Antoine Bourdelle (bronze, France, 1909). Photograph by Carol M. Highsmith (1946–) from the Jon B. Lovelace Collection of California Photographs in *Carol M. Highsmith's America Project* / Library of Congress, Prints and Photographs Division. Public domain.

Figure 23: *Venus and Mars* by Botticelli (paint on canvas, Italy, 1483). "Venus and Mars, c. 1485" painting by Sandro Botticelli (Alessandro di Mariano di Vanni Filipepi). 1444/5-1510 / National Gallery, London, UK / Bridgeman Images. Used with permission.

Figure 24: Immanuel Kant (print, Germany, nineteenth century). Figure from *Meyers Lexicon* by Hermann Julius Meyer. Image from Shutterstock.

Figure 25: *Still Life with Apples* by Cézanne (paint on canvas, France, 1893–94). Painting by Paul Cézanne (1839–1906). Digital image courtesy of the J. Paul Getty Museum's Open Content Program.

Figure 26: *Les Demoiselles d'Avignon* by Picasso (paint on canvas, France, 1907). Painting by Pablo Picasso (1881–1973) / Museum of Modern Art, New York, USA / Bridgeman Images. Used with permission.

Figure 27: *Guernica* by Picasso (paint on canvas, France, 1937). Museo Nacional Centro de Arte Reina Sofía, Madrid, Spain / Bridgeman Images. Used with permission.

Figure 28: Figure from *Pedagogical Sketchbook* by Paul Klee (print, Germany, 1925). Sketches by Paul Klee (1879–1940) from *Pädagogisches Skizzenbuch*, Bauhausbücher No. 2 (Munich: Bauhaus, 1925). Public domain.

Figure 29: *Minotaur* by Picasso (pencil drawing with pasted papers and cloth tacked on wood, France, 1935). *Minotaure*, No. 1 (Paris: Albert Skira, June 1933). From a sketch by Al Burkhardt. Public domain.

Figure 30: Poster for Cabaret Voltaire by Marcel Słodki (print, Switzerland, 1916). Wikimedia Commons.

Figure 31: *The Sacrament of the Last Supper* by Salvador Dalí (paint on canvas, Spain, 1955). Painting by Salvador Dalí (1904–89) / National Gallery of Art, Washington DC, USA / Bridgeman Images. Used with permission.

Figure 32: Noh theater by Torii Kiyomitsu (polychrome woodblock print on paper, Japan, c. 1763). "The Curfew at Dōjōji" by Torii Kiyomitsu (1735–1785). Used with permission of the Metropolitan Museum of Art through a Creative Commons (public domain) license.

Figure 33: *The Lower Depths* by Maxim Gorky (Russia, 1902). Photograph by Ervina Boeve of Moscow Art Theater's premiere of *The Lower Depths*. Wikimedia Commons.

Figure 34: Max Reinhardt's production of *A Midsummer Night's Dream* (United States, 1935). Used with permission of Bridgeman Images.

Figure 35: Michio Ito (France, 1919). "Japanese dancer and choreographer Michio Itō," *Shadowlands*, November 1919. Wikimedia Commons.

Figure 36: Isadora Duncan (United States, c. 1916–18). Photograph by Arnold Genthe. Wikimedia Commons.

Figure 37: Michio Ito as the Hawk in *At the Hawk's Well* (England, c. 1916). Photograph by Alvin Langdon Coburn (1882–1960). Wikimedia Commons.

Figure 38: Isadora Duncan at the Parthenon (Greece, c. 1921). "Isadora Duncan at the Columns of the Parthenon, Athens, 1921" by Edward Steichen (1879–1973). Public domain.

Figure 39: Ruth Dennis as Radha (United States, 1906). From the Jerome Robbins Dance Division, New York Public Library Digital Collections. Accessed September 7, 2017. Public domain.

Figure 40: Raymond Duncan with his wife and child (France, 1912). Photo copyright © PVDE / Bridgeman Images. Used with permission.

Figure 41: *Isadora Duncan* (watercolor and ink on paper, United States, 1915). "Isadora Duncan #29" by Abraham Walkowitz (1878–1965). Gift by the artist to the Brooklyn Museum of Art. Wikimedia Commons.

Figure 42: Michio Ito in *Bushido* (United States, 1916). "Michio Ito wearing fox mask designed by Edmund Dulac," by Alvin Langdon Coburn. Wikimedia Commons.

Figure 43: Rudolf von Laban demonstrating Labanotation (Germany, 1929). Copyright © SZ Photo / Bridgeman Images. Used with permission.

Figure 44: Mary Wigman (Germany, 1922). Photograph by Jacob Merkelbach. Beeldbank Stadsarchief Amsterdam. Wikimedia Commons.

Figure 45: *Totentanz der Mary Wigman* by Ernst Ludwig Kirchner (paint on canvas, Germany, c. 1926–28). Painting by Enrst Ludwig Kirchner (1880–1938). Photo copyright © SZ Photo / Scherl / Bridgeman Images. Used with permission.

Figure 46: *Dancing Mary Wigman* by Ernst Ludwig Kirchner (paint on canvas, Germany, 1933). Painting by Enrst Ludwig Kirchner (1880–1938). Wikimedia Commons.

Figure 47: *Totenmal* (Germany, c. 1930). Photographer unknown. Public domain.

Figure 48: Hanya Holm (England, 1958). "Hanya Holm on March 28, 1958, in London during rehearsal of *My Fair Lady.*" Bridgeman Images. Used with permission.

Figure 49: *Trend* (United States, 1937). Photograph by Barbara Morgan. Used through permission of the Barbara Morgan Archive.

Figure 50: *The Shakers* (United States, 1937). Photograph by Barbara Morgan. Used through permission of the Barbara Morgan Archive.

Figure 51: *Letter to the World* featuring Martha Graham (left) and Jean Erdman (right) (United States, 1945). Photograph by Barbara Morgan. Used through permission of the Barbara Morgan Archive.

Figure 52: Merce Cunningham (right) and company (Iran, 1972). "Shiraz Art Festival, Persepolis Event, Douglas Dunn (left), Carolyn Brown (rear) and Merce Cunningham (far right)." Photo courtesy of Cunningham Dance Foundation archive / Wikimedia Commons.

Figure 53: Jean Erdman in *The Transformations of Medusa* (United States, 1942). Photograph by Barbara Morgan. Used through permission of the Barbara Morgan Archive.

Figure 54: Jean Erdman in *Hamadryad* (United States, 1948). Photograph by Maya Deren.

Figure 55: Jean Erdman with a prop from *Pierrot, the Moon* (India, 1955). Photograph by Joseph Campbell. Copyright © 1995 by Joseph Campbell Foundation (JCF.org). All rights reserved.

Figure 56: *The Coach with the Six Insides* (United States, 1964). Photographer unknown. Copyright © 1964 by Jean Erdman. Used with permission. All rights reserved.

A JOSEPH CAMPBELL BIBLIOGRAPHY

Following are the major books authored and edited by Joseph Campbell. Each entry gives bibliographic data concerning the first edition or, if applicable, the original date of publication along with the bibliographic data for the edition published by New World Library as part of the Collected Works of Joseph Campbell. For information concerning all other editions, please refer to the Complete Works of Joseph Campbell on the Joseph Campbell Foundation website (www.jcf.org).

AUTHOR

Where the Two Came to Their Father: A Navaho War Ceremonial Given by Jeff King. Bollingen Series I. With Maud Oakes and Jeff King. Richmond, VA: Old Dominion Foundation, 1943.

A Skeleton Key to Finnegans Wake: Unlocking James Joyce's Masterwork. With Henry Morton Robinson. 1944. Second edition, Novato, CA: New World Library, 2005.*

The Hero with a Thousand Faces. Bollingen Series XVII. 1949. Third edition, Novato, CA: New World Library, 2008.*

The Masks of God, 4 vols. New York: Viking Press, 1959–1968. Vol. 1, *Primitive Mythology*, 1959. Third edition, Novato, CA: New World Library, 2021.* Vol. 2, *Oriental Mythology*, 1962. Third edition, Novato, CA: New World Library, 2021.* Vol. 3, *Occidental Mythology*, 1964. Third edition, Novato, CA: New World Library, 2021.* Vol. 4, *Creative Mythology*, 1968.

The Flight of the Wild Gander: Explorations in the Mythological Dimension—Selected Essays 1944–1968. 1969. Third edition, Novato, CA: New World Library, 2002.*

Myths to Live By. 1972. Ebook edition, San Anselmo, CA: Joseph Campbell Foundation, 2011.

The Mythic Image. Bollingen Series C. Princeton, NJ: Princeton University
   Press, 1974.
The Inner Reaches of Outer Space: Metaphor as Myth and as Religion. 1986.
   Reprint, Novato, CA: New World Library, 2002.*
Historical Atlas of World Mythology:
   Vol. 1, *The Way of the Animal Powers.* New York: Alfred van der Marck
      Editions, 1983. Reprint in 2 pts. Part 1, *Mythologies of the Primitive
      Hunters and Gatherers.* New York: Alfred van der Marck Editions,
      1988. Part 2, *Mythologies of the Great Hunt.* New York: Alfred van
      der Marck Editions, 1988.
   Vol. 2, *The Way of the Seeded Earth,* 3 pts. Part 1, *The Sacrifice.* New York:
      Alfred van der Marck Editions, 1988. Part 2, *Mythologies of the Primi-
      tive Planters: The Northern Americas.* New York: Harper & Row Pe-
      rennial Library, 1989. Part 3, *Mythologies of the Primitive Planters: The
      Middle and Southern Americas.* New York: Harper & Row Perennial
      Library, 1989.
The Power of Myth. With Bill Moyers. Edited by Betty Sue Flowers. New
   York: Doubleday, 1988.
Transformations of Myth Through Time. New York: Harper & Row, 1990.
The Hero's Journey: Joseph Campbell on His Life and Work. Edited by Phil
   Cousineau. 1990. Reprint, Novato, CA: New World Library, 2003.*
Reflections on the Art of Living: A Joseph Campbell Companion. Edited by
   Diane K. Osbon. New York: HarperCollins, 1991.
Mythic Worlds, Modern Words: On the Art of James Joyce. Edited by Edmund
   L. Epstein. 1993. Second edition, Novato, CA: New World Library,
   2003.*
Baksheesh & Brahman: Asian Journals—India. Edited by Robin Larsen,
   Stephen Larsen, and Antony Van Couvering. 1995. Second edition,
   Novato, CA: New World Library, 2002.* [Reissued in paperback, to-
   gether with *Sake & Satori,* in 2017; see *Asian Journals* entry below.]
The Mythic Dimension: Selected Essays 1959–1987. Edited by Antony Van Cou-
   vering. 1997. Second edition, Novato, CA: New World Library, 2007.*
Thou Art That. Edited by Eugene Kennedy. Novato, CA: New World Li-
   brary, 2001.*
Sake & Satori: Asian Journals—Japan. Edited by David Kudler. Novato, CA:
   New World Library, 2002.* [Reissued in paperback, together with *Baksheesh & Brahman,* in 2017; see *Asian Journals* entry below.]
Myths of Light. Edited by David Kudler. Novato, CA: New World Library,
   2003.*

Pathways to Bliss: Mythology and Personal Transformation. Edited by David
   Kudler. Novato, CA: New World Library, 2004.*
Mythic Imagination: Collected Short Fiction. Novato, CA: New World
   Library, 2012.*
Goddesses: Mysteries of the Feminine Divine. Edited by Safron Rossi. Novato,
   CA: New World Library, 2013.*
Romance of the Grail: The Magic and Mystery of Arthurian Myth. Edited by
   Evans Lansing Smith. Novato, CA: New World Library, 2015.*
Asian Journals: India and Japan. Combined paperback reissue of *Baksheesh
   & Brahman* and *Sake & Satori.* Book I: *Baksheesh & Brahman*—edited
   by Robin Larsen, Stephen Larsen, and Antony Van Couvering; book
   II: *Sake & Satori*—edited by David Kudler. Novato, CA: New World
   Library, 2017.*
The Ecstasy of Being: Mythology and Dance. Edited by Nancy Allison, CMA.
   Novato, CA: New World Library, 2017.*
Correspondence: 1927–1987. Edited by Evans Lansing Smith and Dennis
   Patrick Slattery. Novato, CA: New World Library, 2018.*

*   Published by New World Library as part of the Collected Works of Joseph Campbell.

EDITOR

Books edited and completed from the posthuma of Heinrich Zimmer:
Myths and Symbols in Indian Art and Civilization. Bollingen Series VI. New
   York: Pantheon, 1946.
The King and the Corpse. Bollingen Series XI. New York: Pantheon, 1948.
Philosophies of India. Bollingen Series XXVI. New York: Pantheon, 1951.
The Art of Indian Asia. Bollingen Series XXXIX, 2 vols. New York: Pantheon,
   1955.

Other books edited:
The Portable Arabian Nights. New York: Viking Press, 1951.
Papers from the Eranos Yearbooks. Bollingen Series XXX, 6 vols. Edited with
   R. F. C. Hull and Olga Froebe-Kapteyn. Translated by Ralph Manheim.
   Princeton, NJ: Princeton University Press, 1954–1969.
Myth, Dreams and Religion: Eleven Visions of Connection. New York: E. P.
   Dutton, 1970.
The Portable Jung. By C. G. Jung. Translated by R. F. C. Hull. New York:
   Viking Press, 1971.
My Life and Lives. By Rato Khyongla Nawang Losang. New York: E. P. Dut-
   ton, 1977.

INDEX

Page references followed by *fig.* indicate illustrations or material contained in their captions.

ABOUT THE AUTHOR

———————•———————

JOSEPH CAMPBELL was an American author and teacher best known for his work in the field of comparative mythology. He was born in New York City in 1904, and in early childhood became interested in mythology. He loved to read books about American Indian cultures and frequently visited the American Museum of Natural History in New York, where he was fascinated by the museum's collection of totem poles. Campbell was educated at Columbia University, where he specialized in medieval literature, and, after earning a master's degree, continued his studies at universities in Paris and Munich. While abroad he was influenced by the art of Pablo Picasso and Henri Matisse, the novels of James Joyce and Thomas Mann, and the psychological studies of Sigmund Freud and Carl Jung. These encounters led to Campbell's theory that all myths and epics are linked in the human psyche, and that they are cultural manifestations of the universal need to explain social, cosmological, and spiritual realities.

After a period in California, where he encountered John Steinbeck and the biologist Ed Ricketts, Campbell taught at the Canterbury School, and then, in 1934, joined the literature department at Sarah Lawrence College, a post he retained for many years. During the 1940s and '50s, he helped Swami

239

Nikhilananda to translate the Upaniṣads and *The Gospel of Sri Ramakrishna*. He also edited works by the German scholar Heinrich Zimmer on Indian art, myths, and philosophy.

In 1944, with Henry Morton Robinson, Campbell published *A Skeleton Key to Finnegans Wake*. His first original work, *The Hero with a Thousand Faces*, came out in 1949 and was immediately well received; in time, it became acclaimed as a classic. In this study of the "myth of the hero," Campbell asserted that there is a single pattern of heroic journey and that all cultures share this essential pattern in their various heroic myths. In his book he also outlined the basic conditions, stages, and results of the archetypal hero's journey.

Joseph Campbell died in 1987. In 1988 a series of television interviews with Bill Moyers, *The Power of Myth*, introduced Campbell's views to millions of people.

ABOUT THE
JOSEPH CAMPBELL FOUNDATION

———•———

THE JOSEPH CAMPBELL FOUNDATION (JCF) is a not-for-profit corporation that continues the work of Joseph Campbell, exploring the fields of mythology and comparative religion. The Foundation is guided by three principal goals:

First, the Foundation preserves, protects, and perpetuates Campbell's pioneering work. This includes cataloging and archiving his works, developing new publications based on his works, directing the sale and distribution of his published works, protecting copyrights to his works, and increasing awareness of his works by making them available in digital formats on JCF's website.

Second, the Foundation furthers his pioneering work in mythology and comparative religion. This involves promoting the study of mythology and comparative religion, implementing and/or supporting diverse mythological education programs, supporting and/or sponsoring events designed to increase public awareness, donating Campbell's archived works to the New York Public Library and his personal library to OPUS Archive & Research Center, and utilizing JCF's website (www.jcf.org) as a forum for mythologically informed cross-cultural dialogue.

Third, the Foundation helps individuals enrich their lives by participating in a series of programs, including our global, Internet-based Associates program; our local international network of Mythological Roundtables; and our periodic Joseph Campbell–related events and activities.

For more information on Joseph Campbell
and the Joseph Campbell Foundation, contact:
Joseph Campbell Foundation
www.jcf.org